2

NATIVE AMERICAN COURTSHIP AND MARRIAGE TRADITIONS

Other books of interest from Hippocrene . . .

Scottish Tartan Weddings: A Practical Guidebook
180 pages • 5¹/₂ x 8¹/₂ • illustrations • 0-7818-0754-9
• $22.50hc • (353)

Polish Wedding Customs and Traditions
196 pages • 6 x 9 • photos/illustrations • 0-7818-0530-9
• $19.95hc • (641)

Under the Wedding Canopy: Love and Marriage in Judaism
243 pages • 5¹/₂ x 8¹/₂ • 0-7818-0481-7 • $22.50hc • (596)

I Do, I Do: American Wedding Etiquette of Yesteryear
228 pages • 6 x 9 • 0-7818-0650-X • $19.95hc • (730)

Treasury of Wedding Poems, Quotations & Short Stories
142 pages • 6 x 9 • 0-7818-0636-4 • $17.50hc • (729)

Native American Language titles from Hippocrene . . .

Navajo-English Dictionary
9,000 entries • 164 pages • 5¹/₂ x 8¹/₂ • 0-7818-0278-4
• $9.95pb • (223)

Colloquial Navajo: A Dictionary
10,000 entries • 461 pages • 5¹/₂ x 8¹/₂ • 0-7818-0278-4
• $16.95pb • (282)

Yoeme-English/English-Yoeme Standard Dictionary
A language of the Yaqui Tribe
351 pages • 5¹/₂ x 8¹/₂ • 0-7818-0663-X • $16.95pb • (713)

All prices subject to change without prior notice. To purchase Hippocrene Books contact your local bookstore, call (718) 454-2366, or write to: HIPPOCRENE BOOKS, 171 Madison Avenue, New York, NY 10016. Please enclose check or money order, adding $5.00 shipping (UPS) for the first book and $.50 for each additional book.

NATIVE AMERICAN COURTSHIP AND MARRIAGE TRADITIONS

BY

LESLIE GOURSE

Hippocrene Books, Inc.
New York

Acknowledgments

Cover photo of Navajo wedding © 1995 Susanne Page. Used by permission.

"The Legend of the Flute" and "The Serpent of the Sea" from AMERICAN INDIAN MYTHS AND LEGENDS by Richard Erdoes and Alfonso Ortiz.
Copyright © 1984 by Richard Erdoes and Alfonso Ortiz.
Reprinted by permission of Pantheon Books, a division of Random House, Inc.

3 recipes: "Mushrooms Stuffed with Salmon," "Maple-Mustard Vinaigrette" and "Frybread" from NEW NATIVE AMERICAN COOKING by Dale Carson.
Copyright © 1996 by Dale Carson. Reprinted by permission of Random House, Inc.

ISBN 0-7818-0768-9

For information, address:
HIPPOCRENE BOOKS, INC.
171 Madison Avenue
New York, NY 10016

Cataloging-in-Publication Data available from the Library of Congress.

Printed in the United States of America.

TABLE OF CONTENTS

~ 1 ~

OVERVIEW AND INTRODUCTION 1

~ 2 ~

LITERATURE—LOVE POEMS AND FOLKLORE 21

~ ~

INTRODUCTION TO TRIBAL WEDDING CUSTOMS 49

~ 3 ~

TRIBAL WEDDING CUSTOMS—THE HOPI 53

~ 4 ~

TRIBAL WEDDING CUSTOMS—THE NAVAJO 61

~ 5 ~

TRIBAL WEDDING CUSTOMS—
    THE STORY OF AN EASTERN CHEROKEE BRIDE
    AND A MINNESOTA SIOUX BRIDEGROOM 69

~ 6 ~

TRIBAL WEDDING CUSTOMS—THE IROQUOIS 75

~ 7 ~

TRIBAL WEDDING CUSTOMS—THE OGLALA SIOUX 81

⌒ 8 ⌒

CELEBRATIONS OF PUBERTY 91

⌒ 9 ⌒

DANCES AND POWWOWS .115

⌒ 10 ⌒

FOOD 129

⌒ 11 ⌒

FASHIONS, JEWELRY, BASKETRY, CLOTH WEAVING,
    AND DECORATIONS 148

POST SCRIPT—DIVORCE AND REMARRIAGE 159

BIBLIOGRAPHY AND INFORMATION RESOURCES 163

INDEX 167

1

OVERVIEW
AND
INTRODUCTION

Pocahontas, the favorite daughter of a great Powhatan chief in the territory that would become known as Virginia, contracted a unique marriage for her era on April 5, 1614. In a Christian ceremony, she and Englishman John Rolfe, a tobacco farmer, were married by the senior minister of a Jamestown church. Pocahontas was nineteen years old—already old for a Powhatan Indian maiden to marry. She wore an English wedding dress of fine muslin and a long veil and robe, and around her neck, a string of freshwater pearls—a wedding gift from her father, Chief Powhatan (as the English called him.)

Her uncle, a chief of his own village, and two of her brothers attended the wedding. Powhatan, leader of all the Powhatan villages, refused to go himself. The English believed he didn't want to give anyone the impression that he was surrendering his rights to his land in any way. He and the English had fought many battles, and now he simply wanted to live without wars. He knew he couldn't drive the English away from his territories. And he accepted his daughter's choice of a husband. But he was keeping his distance from the English and maintaining his dignity as a chief by staying away from the wedding ceremony. To him, as well as to the English, the marriage symbolized a type of business deal, as the best Indian marriages always did.

To show his enduring love for his daughter, Powhatan gave the newlyweds some land north of Jamestown on the James River. The couple built a house there and named it "Varina" in honor of the Spanish word for the type of tobacco Rolfe grew.

The governor of Jamestown visited Powhatan one day. The old chief asked him how Pocahontas and Rolfe "lived, loved, and liked." The governor told Powhatan that the couple was very happy. He seemed pleased and peaceful in his old age. Though the English and the Powhatans still engaged in little skirmishes occasionally, they traded with each other and coexisted. People referred to the time as the Peace of Pocahontas. So the unusual alliance between an Indian princess and a British farmer had great political ramifications.

Probably nobody but Pocahontas, always a very bright and curious child, could have become involved in such a marriage at that time. She had enjoyed a special relationship with the English from the day the first boat landed on Powhatan land. A pre-adolescent girl accustomed to running around without any clothes—Powhatan girls didn't dress in their doeskin skirts until they reached puberty—she became friendly with Captain John Smith, a prominent member of the English expedition. Many times their friendship helped save the lives of the English settlers suffering gruesome hardships, particularly famine and disease, in a strange land. Pocahontas persuaded her father to give corn and small game to the English countless times.

Eventually, John Smith had a serious accident; Pocahontas, by then a young lady in a doeskin skirt, with decorative feathers in her hair, mistakenly believed he was dead. He returned to England without saying good-bye to her. She refused to marry an Indian man whom her father wanted her to choose, and she went to live with a relative in a distant village. An Englishman visiting there was surprised to see her. The English didn't know where she had gone. He invited her to have dinner on his boat; when she arrived, he locked her in a room and sailed with her to James-town. The Englishman had the bright idea to use her as a pawn in a power struggle and bribe her father to do favors for the English in return for his beloved daughter's release. But the wily Powhatan resisted. He guessed correctly that the English were very grateful to Pocahontas for all the kindnesses and favors she had done for them; they would treat her well.

Unable to budge her father, the English soon released her from her jail cell. A minister of the Church of England, Reverend Alexander Whittaker, who respected Indians, took her to live in his house. He converted her to Christianity—some say she made the decision of her own free will.

Instructed to behave like an English lady, she put away her Indian doeskin skirt, beads, and feathers in a closet. Instead she wore a stiff corset made with whalebones, and on top of that she put on a blouse that covered her upper body all the way to her neck; she also wore an ankle-length skirt to conform to English fashion.

She was taught to bow her head down and look at the ground when she walked in the streets the way Englishwomen did. Fluent in English, she learned to read Christian prayers. The English sent word to King James I in England that an Indian princess had chosen to convert to Christianity. Religious conversions had been one of the major missions of the

English. She became known by her baptismal name, Rebecca.

However, Pocahontas wasn't simply a pawn or a prized possession. The English truly liked her for her delightful personality. One Sunday in church, a widower named John Rolfe noticed her and began talking with her, calling her Pocahontas out of respect for her background. Furthermore, he found himself very attracted to the small, dark woman with delicate hands.

Every free moment he had, John Rolfe visited her at Reverend Whittaker's farm. He sat with her in church on Sundays, took walks with her in the tobacco fields, and talked about the beauty of the land. Pocahontas liked Rolfe, too, for his sweet, respectful personality and his curiosity about people and places. Rolfe wanted to marry her and asked the governor of Jamestown whether marriage with a woman who had been born a "heathen" would be acceptable.

The governor was very pleased. He thought the English and Indians distrusted each other because of their struggle for control of the land, and a marriage between a colonist and an Indian princess could ameliorate tensions between the English and the Indians. The governor also hoped that the marriage would encourage more English people to venture to the New World and, most especially, to send more money.

It remained for Pocahontas, her fiancé Rolfe, and other settlers to go to Powhatan's village and ask for his blessing for the marriage. Instead of meeting the boat, Powhatan sent two of his sons, who delivered the message that Powhatan approved of the marriage. He wanted better relations with the English. "I'm tired of fighting," he said.

If there is one thing that this marriage had in common with most marriages between Indians with Indians, and which undoubtedly led Powhatan to accept the match, it was the nature of the gifts exchanged by the couple—Powhatan's gift of a little of his land to the newlyweds in return for a peaceful attitude from the English colonists.

Pocahontas/Rebecca lived in the English style. A year after her marriage, she had a baby son, whom she named Thomas in honor of the English governor. Jamestown's financial backers felt so delighted that they set up a financial award as a way of thanking Pocahontas for all the help she had given the colony to ensure its survival in past years; every year the fund paid Pocahontas and her son. She did maintain some of her Indian traditions in her daily life in the farmhouse which she and John Rolfe built on the land her father had given them on the shore of the James river. She sang Indian lullabies to her son, tied him to a crib board in the Indian fashion, and propped him up against a wall. That way she could keep an eye on him while she did her chores.

Eventually she traveled to England, where she met the colony's financial backers in the Virginia Company, and they presented her to the King and Queen at court. Captain John Smith, whom she had believed was dead, paid her a surprise visit in the inn where she was staying. By that time she was weak from an illness—probably pneumonia. His visit excited and agitated her tremendously. She was actually overwhelmed by emotion, because she had been so attached to him. Though she had been only an adolescent when she met him, she had probably fallen in love with him. She was certainly very angry to learn he was alive and had simply never contacted her. She died of pneumonia and was buried in England. Her son, who was raised there by his father's relatives, didn't return to Jamestown until he was a grown man. Both the English and the Indians trusted him, as they had Pocahontas.

Although marriages between Indians and white settlers of European backgrounds did take place as years went on, they never became everyday events. Usually they met with none of the acceptance and entailed none of the rituals and ceremonies that marriages between Indians in their close-knit tribes did. Furthermore, well-defined Indian marriage traditions and rites had little in common with those of the Europeans.

Had Pocahontas married an Indian, her father would have received a request for her hand in marriage from a suitable young man—in this case a brave, smart man whom an Indian chief could be proud to have as his son-in-law. The families would meet to exchange gifts. The gifts from the bride's family, if it had means—and Powhatan certainly did—would usually equal the value and even surpass the sumptuousness of the gifts from the groom's people. Indians usually made horses a major gift item in the marriage agreements. In many tribes, when the families exchanged gifts, the couple became formally married. Then the families relaxed with a feast, its lavishness dependent upon the means of the bride's and groom's immediate families and their relatives. (Relatives sometimes added to the bride prices and the feast foods.) Events leading up to the marriages, from early courtship days, and continuing through the rest of the lives of the couples, were usually well prescribed in the varied customs and traditions of the different tribes. Some parents even contracted marriages, at least informally, when the future brides were still babies, and their prospective husbands were already young boys.

Four centuries of American history have eroded the systems that the Indians so carefully worked out and practiced faithfully. These days, most Native American couples who decide to get married simply seek out a clergyman or a Justice of the Peace or they go to City Hall, as many others in the country do. Rarely do Native Americans delve into their rich heritage of customs and ceremonies about courtship, marriage and family structure. "They're gone," says an Indian woman, who works at the Smithsonian Institution's National Museum of the American Indian in New York. Only the people of the Long House—the Iroquois—and a few Western tribes keep some of their traditions alive, and the Iroquois do it more or less secretly. (Though Indians all around the country stage powwows regularly and invite the public, they still have some private celebrations to which they don't welcome non-Indians.) Otherwise the Native American marriage traditions are relegated to the memories of older people and the history books.

Some books, articles, sociological and anthropological treatises written by experts on Indian history help keep the memories alive. Indians themselves have delivered oral histories about their lives, including courtship, marriage, and related arrangements and rites. One reason so many sources exist is that there have been so many tribes, and the regions in which they have lived necessitated different survival tactics. So legend and lore and factual accounts vary greatly from region to region and tribe to tribe. Often experts have concentrated on one tribe or region—the eastern tribes, for example, or the southwestern tribes—and have studied their different mating and marriage traditions. Similarities between them have also emerged, for all the tribes have shared some concerns, traditions, and history.

Here are a few examples of common characteristics of Native American family, courtship, and marriage traditions.

In general, marriages were arranged by parents who wanted to merge the worldly goods of two families; sometimes these families were already related. It was common for a mother with a son, and her brother with a daughter, to have her son marry her brother's daughter. That was considered a good arrangement— and better than having the son marry the daughter of the mother's sister. But incest—a marriage between a brother and sister, or between a father and daughter, for example—was strictly forbidden, and even punishable by death. The rules and regulations about family relationships could be extremely complex. But once the Indians were satisfied that a couple had a right to be married, the families conducted their usual business dealings to seal the marriage promises.

Usually the men did the hunting and fishing, while the women built their houses—tipis, hogans, or huts— and raised children, cooked for the family, and made clothes, tools, and utensils for the household.

Some tribes practiced polygamy. About half of all marriages of the Blackfoot tribe were polygamous, because so many men were killed in battle, and women outnumbered men by two and three to one. Occasionally—and very rarely—in some tribes, the woman had two husbands. More often a husband had two or more wives—and sometimes the wives were sisters or other close relatives. If a woman was widowed, her husband's brother was supposed to marry her, whether he was married already or not. In a non-polygamous tribe or marriage, if a woman died, the widower was sometimes expected to marry a sister of his late wife.

Even in tribes that practiced polygamy, not all the marriages were polygamous. Many were monogamous. Arrangements depended upon what a husband could afford—how many wives and children he could feed. In some tribes only the chief was polygamous. Powhatan, for example, had many wives.

Indian families were often, though not exclusively, matrilineal; the property was passed down through the women. And if a woman wanted to divorce a man, she could do so rather easily by dropping his possessions outside the door. There were variations on the divorce rites, including child custody traditions.

A Navajo legend, which was passed down from ancient days, said that a man and woman had fought about sex. The man claimed that the woman was too interested in sex. As a result of the quarrel, all the men took their rafts and moved across the river, where they destroyed their rafts. Living separately, both the men and women suffered the tortures of the damned. For one thing, they were dying out. So the women asked the men to return. When they did, the men and women agreed that the man should lead the way about sexual matters, since men were the stronger sex. But they absolutely needed each other for survival in many ways. They complemented each other, and, unable to exist without each other, they achieved a kind of equality, with neither sex living in slavery or subservience to the other.

So women were never considered to be the property or chattel of men, although Europeans coming upon Indian cultures might have mistakenly thought so. The behavior of Indians could mislead the whites. Blackfoot Indians sometimes were very cruel and could do whatever they liked to their wives. But a truly abused Blackfoot wife could go back to her own family, whether her husband objected or not.

Indians tended to marry young. In some tribes, girls married soon after they began to menstruate. In other tribes, they married a few years later. Different tribes dealt with their young, marriageable females in a variety of ways. Some tribes went so far as to isolate young women indoors until they were married. Most tribes encouraged at least some separation of the sexes—and sometimes very strict separation—until marriage.

Tribes sponsored dances and ceremonies at which young men and women could meet, sometimes only once a year, to choose their mates. The youngsters weren't supposed to talk much with each other at such events. The girls were taught to be modest, quiet, and virginal, and to some degree virginity in a bride was valued in many tribes.

But Indians, or at least the majority of Indian tribes, didn't place impossible demands on their young, sexually excitable adolescents. Young couples found many ways to arrange clandestine meetings. In hunting and gathering tribes, the women were supposed to fetch water and firewood. So when they went to the springs, streams, or the woods around their camps, young men arranged to meet or at least see their loved ones. Lovers also found berry picking times ideal for rendezvous away from the watchful eyes of older people. Indians considered flute music to be particularly seductive. So young men composed and played tunes on their flutes for their lovers. When a girl heard a special tune, she knew her lover was nearby.

In addition to flute music and food, young people used magic charms as lures and cast spells over their beloveds—both for good and evil. The love potions of the Cree tribe were supposed to be so powerful that other tribes, such as the Blackfoot, referred to magic charms as Cree medicine. Popular with the Blackfoot was the practice of carving the image of a man and a woman out of birch bark. Then a stick was dipped in a magic potion, and the hearts of the figurines were touched by the stick. The magic trick was supposed to be irresistible. A woman might not have welcomed the advances of a man, but after her figurine's heart was touched by the magic potion, she fell in love with him.

If she decided she wanted a particular man for her husband, in some tribes a woman prepared a special type of food for him and invited him to a picnic. If he wasn't interested, he turned down the invitation, for he knew what was in the picnic basket.

In some tribes, a young woman was expected to marry the first man she had sexual intercourse with, and in other tribes a young woman was supposed to experiment sexually and gain experience. But in most tribes, a woman could expect retribution if she stole another woman's husband or committed adultery after marriage.

Some couples decided to elope; if they did, they had to hide themselves, at least for a while, to escape punishment. But they could show up together as a married couple at the next harvest (that was one ideal time) and they were accepted. Then their families exchanged the usual presents at the proper level for their social status. Elopement wasn't a serious offense in any tribe, though some tribes approved of it less than others did.

Young people could enjoy a variety of traditional, seductive courtship rites. The Navajo tribe held a squaw dance, which was, in a sense, something like a debutante ball, where parents showed off their marriageable daughters. Young men appeared with their best horses or wagons, and girls bedecked themselves with jewelry—fertility symbols, such as squash blossom necklaces, in some cases, and beads, shells, and feathers in their hair—and clothes they had made or borrowed for the occasion. Navajo girls could choose their own dance partners and expect the young men to give presents. The women could be very bold, if they chose, to the extent that they might even lead a boy off into the bushes. Some Navajo parents didn't let their daughters attend the squaw dances, because of their freewheeling nature. But in general the Navajos were open-minded about premarital sex.

From their older, female relatives, young women got plenty of advice about courtship and marriage when they started menstruating; they found ways to put the counsel to good use when they spent their days tending sheep—and had clandestine meetings with their boyfriends. (A Navajo girl was considered a virgin unless she said she wasn't one, or unless she was caught in the sex act.)

Many tribes had a tradition called nightcrawling. A young man would wait until a village fell silent, then creep into his beloved's lodge or tipi and stay with her all night; at daybreak he crept away and returned to his own home. In some tribes, the man simply slipped his hand under a tipi and held onto his beloved, sometimes grabbing her genitals. If the woman didn't accept the man, she might scream, and he could be caught and punished. In some tribes, parents built shelves above their beds and made their daughters sleep there. That stopped the young men from nightcrawling successfully.

While nightcrawling was a general practice, different tribes had sharply divergent opinions about it. The Hopis accepted it as normal. But the strict Apaches thought it was dishonorable, and if they caught a man in the act, they might beat him and destroy his property. Some tribes absolutely forbade any socializing between girls and boys at all until they were married. One Northwestern tribe actually sent its adolescent girls to live separately from the rest of the tribe. The practice kept the girls virginal and very light-skinned, not only away from young men but out of the sun's rays and away from all of life's usual experiences. Some tribes isolated their young women only when they were menstruating, brainwashing the girls with fables and superstitions about the terrible consequences of a woman socializing with anyone when she had her period. The tales frequently terrified young women. But these tribes devised happy celebrations for women at menarche, the onset of their periods.

In tribes that kept young people divided by sex, the psychological transition for newlyweds was difficult. Adults devised many ways to help young couples adapt to married life. Some couples spent a year living with their parents, often the bride's parents, before setting up their own lodge. Some bridegrooms worked for their wives' families for a period of time and even lived with their wives' families before the couple began to have sexual relations. Some couples didn't live together, but each stayed with his or her own family until they had children of their own to raise. And in some tribes, the bridegrooms, though expected to be respectful, weren't allowed to look directly at their mother-in-laws or have any contact with them except in dire emergencies. The reasons for that custom are complex, but it often helped young couples achieve a degree of domestic harmony and peace without interference from older people.

In every tribe, girls married young, having learned to make their own clothes and costumes for weddings and other occasions. In the southwestern tribes, however, older male relatives wove wedding dresses for the brides. The brides often kept the dresses to serve as their burial robes, too. In the Hopi tribe, the brides had two dresses prepared for their weddings—one for the wedding day, and another for their burial.

Their husbands were supposed to hunt and supply the food. In the cases of the warring, western tribes, where the men put themselves at great risk and often died during the hunt or in battle, their widowed wives married many times—but unless the widows were very young, never with all the mighty preparations of the first marriages. Spinsters were virtually unheard of.

Helpful Hints for Bringing Old Traditions Into Contemporary Life:

YOUNG couples want their families to get to know and like each other and to celebrate their joys and comfort each other in difficult times. But once a couple decides to get married, it's a very good idea for them to keep in mind how Indians believed that young couples found peace and harmony if they kept a certain distance from their parents. Remember to think for yourselves and not simply adopt the ideas of your parents, no matter how much you love them or how well-meaning you know them to be. Couples must live independent lives together as new families with their own standards, hopes, and goals.

If you are having difficulties in convincing another person that you are the man or woman he or she should choose over everyone else, you can carve or buy little figurines, take them to dinner with the object of your heart's desire, and touch each of the figurines' hearts with a drop of wine. Explain that the Blackfoot and the Cree Indians did that sort of thing all the time. Of course, perform this little ceremony with a light-hearted smile and a carefree manner. It's the thought that counts if you want to bewitch someone with your charm and wit.

2

LITERATURE—
LOVE POEMS AND
FOLKLORE

There is a wealth of fascinating and beautiful Native American literature that has been passed down and collected through centuries past. Here are some love poems that provide a glimpse of the profound longing and romantic feelings of young Native American lovers, the conditions under which they lived, and the traditions that ruled their lives. The poems shed light on the courtship and marriage-related practices of various tribes. And the poems make it clear that the Indians, despite their technical classification as primitive people, had the same universally complex relationships with each other that all lovers have had from ancient Egypt to contemporary Paris.

Indian poems had their roots in the songs and chants of tribal life. The Indians almost never intended their songs to be entertainment or an expression of a sensitive individual's unique soul. The Indians sang and wrote songs for practical purposes, to conquer or at least deal with the invisible forces in their lives. Songs inspired Indians to conduct their lives honorably and helped them through times of great emotion and need.

A scholar named F.W. Hodge made an astute observation of the role of poetry in the lives of American Indians: "Most Indian rituals can be classed as poetry. (The poems) always relate to serious subjects and are expressed in dignified language, and the words chosen to clothe the thought generally make rhythm . . . The picturesque quality of Indian speech lends itself to poetic conceits and expressions. The few words of a song will, to the Indian, portray a cosmic belief, present the mystery of death, or evoke the memory of joy or grief; to him the terse words project the thought or emotion from the background of his tribal life and experience, and make a song vibrant with poetic meaning. Many of the rites observed among the natives from the Arctic Ocean to the Gulf of Mexico are highly poetic in their significance, symbolism and ceremonial movements; the rituals and accompanying acts, the songs whose rhythm is accentuated by the waving of feathered emblems, the postures and marches, and the altar decorations combine to make up dramas of deep significance, replete with poetic thought and expression."[1]

In short, Indians usually invented songs with a strong purpose clearly in mind—for one thing, to compel love, and sometimes to express simple joy and a spirit of fun, as well as to praise the gods and ask for help, or to explain life and history, and express feelings about enemies and oneself, or to quiet children, or accompany work, or enliven games—all sorts of activities and ideas that were part of daily life. With songs and poetry, Indians explained the world to themselves.

The first selection suggests the elusiveness of opportunities for young lovers to meet each other, the shyness of the young girls, and the yearning for romantic encounters. This one reflects the boy's point of view.

"HER SHADOW"[2]
(from the Ojibwa Tribe)

Out on the lake my canoe is gliding,
Paddle dipping soft lest she should take alarm;
Ah, hey-ah hey-ah ho, hey-ah hey-ah ho, thus I go!
Somewhere along shore she is hiding,
She is shy to yield to love's alluring charm;
Ah, hey-ah hey-ah ho, hey-ah hey-ah, love will win,
    I know.

There is a shadow swiftly stealing!
Should it be her own, soon I will win the race:
Ah hey-ah hey-ah ho, hey-ah hey-ah ho, I think
    it is!
Will she but turn, herself revealing,
I will shout aloud when-e'er I see her face.
Ah! hey-ah hey-ah ho, hey-ah hey-ah ho,
There she is!

⤳ ⤳

A second selection reveals one way that young
lovers found privacy. Sometimes a young woman sat
outside her family's tipi or lodgings and entertained
her boyfriend under a blanket that hid the couple
from the prying eyes of their families and neighbors.
Sometimes, too, young women entertained more than
one young man this way, one after the other, during
the days when the youngsters were getting to know
each other and preparing to choose mates. This poem,
too, expresses the boy's outlook.

"LOVER'S WOOING" or "BLANKET SONG"[2]
(from the Zuni Tribe)

I.
O what happiness!
How delightful,

When together we
'Neath one blanket walk.
We together
'Neath one blanket walk,
We together
'Neath one blanket walk,
We walk.
O! What happiness!
How delightful,
When together we
'Neath one blanket walk.
We together,
'Neath one blanket walk,
We together,
'Neath one blanket walk.
We walk.

II.
Can it be that
My young maiden fair
Sits awaiting,
All alone tonight?
Is she waiting
For me only?
Is she waiting
For me only?

III.
May I hope it is
My young maiden
Sitting all alone
And awaiting me;
Will she come then?
Will she walk with me?
'Neath one blanket
We together be,
We — we two, we two,
We two, we two —
Will she come?

The third and fourth selections express the girl's emotional outlook.

"LOVE SONG"
(from the Dakota Tribe)[2]

Many are the youths, many youths:
Thou alone art he who pleaseth me.
Over all I love thee.
Long shall be the years of parting!

"THE BRIDE'S SONG"
(from the Algonquin Tribe)[2]

There are many men in the world,
But only one is dear to me.
He is good and brave and strong.
He swore to love none but me;
He has forgotten me.
It was an evil spirit that changed him,
But I will love none but him.

⌒　⌒

Both of the last two selections are poignant songs.
Does the first one from the woman's point of view suggest that the young woman will not be marrying the
man she loves and will spend all her life missing him?
For a variety of reasons, it sometimes happened that
young women didn't marry the men they favored
most. Sometimes a girl's family vetoed a girl's selection and asked her to look further for a husband. That
is just one possibility about the inspiration for this
lament.

The second one suggests that a woman has lost her
husband's affection because he has succumbed to the
magic potions, herbs and other concoctions that
Indians loved to use to charm and bedevil each other.

This lament doesn't mean that the woman has lost the love of her husband forever; she might use a potion herself and woo him back. Sometimes potions and the games and havoc they wreaked in the lives of lovers were simply part of the mating game, and true love could win out.

The following two poems are filled with the complexities of the Indians' love lives. The first comes from Frances Densmore's collection, *Poems from Sioux and Chippewa Songs*. Densmore, a piano teacher and church organist, began visiting the Chippewa and Sioux tribes during her vacations, and she started notating the songs she heard. She went on to prepare many publications and became a highly regarded collector, translator, and authoritative commentator about Indian poems.

"I SIT HERE THINKING OF HER"[3]

I sit here thinking of her;
I am sad as I think of her.
Come, I beseech you, let us sing;
Why are you offended?

I do not care for you any more;
Someone else is in my thoughts.

You desire vainly that I seek you;
The reason is, I come to see your younger sister.

Come, let us drink.

〜 〜

"I AM ARRAYED LIKE THE ROSES"[3]

What are you saying to me?
I am arrayed like the roses
And beautiful as they.

I can charm the man.
He is completely fascinated by me

In the center of the earth
Wherever he may be
or under the earth.

〜 〜

The first clearly addresses one man's change of
heart. It might also be interpreted to suggest that one
man, marrying sisters, finds he favors the younger
sister—certainly not a situation that would promote
domestic harmony in a polygamous marriage. The
truth is that polygamous marriages often promoted

jealousies between the sisters who were supposed to provide an ideal arrangement for one husband. Densmore reportedly observed that Indians didn't write many love songs until white people came to North America, and when the Indians did write love songs, or poems, they expressed sorrow and unhappiness more often than the simple joy of love relationships.

The second poem suggests that a woman has used a love potion to bewitch a man. Indians had a wide variety of magic talismans to try to guide the course of their lives. Furthermore, Indians tended to feel uneasy about love charms, since they were used to gain control over other people. But to the contemporary reader, this poem can be interpreted as a straightforward boast of self confidence by a woman happily in love with a man who, she knows, loves her. It would be an ideal poem to work into a contemporary marriage ceremony.

So would the following poem:

"THE HEART'S FRIEND"
(Shoshone Love Song)[4]

Fair is the white star of twilight,
And the sky clearer
At the day's end;
But she is fairer, and she is dearer,
She, my heart's friend!

Fair is the white star of twilight,
and the moon roving to the sky's end;
But she is fairer, better worth loving,
She, my heart's friend.

⌒ ⌒

Native American legends and myths have existed
for thousands of years and are still relevant to today's
world. Many stories are moral tales about human-
kind's relationship with the natural world, but there
are certainly moving and poetic tales about love and
the ritual of courtship. Here are two love stories from
a wonderfully diverse and comprehensive anthology
that readers interested in Native American tradition
should not miss, *American Indian Myths and Legends.*[5]

"THE LEGEND OF THE FLUTE"
(from the Brule Sioux)

Well, you know our flutes; you've heard their
sound and seen how beautifully they are made. That
flute of ours, the *siyotanka*, is for only one kind of
music—love music. In the old days the men would sit
by themselves, maybe lean hidden, unseen, against a
tree in the dark of night. They would make up their
own special tunes, their courting songs.

We Indians are shy. Even if he was a warrior who had already counted coup on an enemy, a young man might hardly screw up courage enough to talk to a nice-looking *winchinchala*—a girl he was in love with. Also, there was no place where a young man and girl could be alone inside the village. The family tipi was always crowded with people. And naturally, you couldn't just walk out of the village hand in hand with your girl, even if hand holding had been one of our customs, which it wasn't. Out there in the tall grass and sagebrush you could be gored by a buffalo, clawed by a grizzly, or tomahawked by a Pawnee, or you could run into the Mila Hanska, the Long Knives, namely the U.S. Cavalry.

The only chance you had to meet your *winchin-chala* was to wait for her at daybreak when the women went to the river or brook with their skin bags to get water. When the girl you had your eye on finally came down the water trail, you popped up from behind some bush and stood so she could see you. And that was about all you could do to show her that you were interested—standing there grinning, looking at your moccasins, scratching your ear, maybe.

The *winchinchala* didn't do much either, except get red in the face, giggle, maybe throw a wild turnip at you. If she liked you, the only way she would let you know was to take her time filling her water bag and peek at you a few times over her shoulder.

So the flutes did the talking. At night, lying on her buffalo robe in her parents' tipi, the girl would hear that moaning, crying sound of the *siyotanka*. By the way it was played, she would know that it was her lover who was out there someplace. And if the elk medicine was very strong in him and her, maybe she would sneak out to follow that sound and meet him without anybody noticing it.

The flute is always made of wood from a cedar tree. In shape it describes the long neck and head of a bird with an open beak. The sound comes out of the beak, and that's where the legend comes in, the legend of how the Lakota people acquired the flute.

Once many generations ago, the people had drums, gourd rattles, and bull-roarers, but no flutes. At that long-ago time a young man went out to hunt. Meat was scarce, and the people in his camp were hungry. He found the tracks of an elk and followed them for a long time. The elk, wise and swift, is the one who owns the love charm. If a man possesses elk medicine, the girl he likes can't help sleeping with him. He will also be a lucky hunter. This young man I'm talking about had no elk medicine.

After many hours he finally sighted his game. He was skilled with bow and arrows, and had a fine new bow and quiver full of straight, well-feathered, flint-tipped arrows. Yet the elk always managed to stay just out of range, leading him on and on. The young man was so intent on following his prey that he hardly noticed where he went.

When night came, he found himself deep inside a thick forest. The tracks had disappeared and so had the elk, and there was no moon. He realized that he was lost and that it was too dark to find his way out. Luckily he came upon a stream with cool, clear water. And he had been careful enough to bring a hide bag of *wansa*—dried meat pounded with berries and kidney fat—strong food that will keep a man going for a few days. After he had drunk and eaten, he rolled himself into his fur robe, propped his back against a tree, and tried to rest. But he couldn't sleep; the forest was full of strange noises, the cries of night animals, the hooting of owls, the groaning of trees in the wind. It was as if he heard these sounds for the first time.

Suddenly there was an entirely new sound, of a kind neither he nor anyone else had ever heard before. It was mournful and ghost-like. It made him afraid, so that he drew his robe tightly about himself and reached for his bow to make sure that it was properly strung. On the other hand, the sound was like a song, sad but beautiful, full of love, hope and yearning. Then before he knew it, he was asleep. He dreamed that the bird called *wagnuka*, the redheaded woodpecker, appeared singing the strangely beautiful song and telling him: "Follow me and I will teach you."

When the hunter awoke, the sun was already high. On a branch of the tree against which he was leaning, he saw a redheaded woodpecker. The bird flew away to another tree, and another, but never very far, looking back all the time at the young man as if to say: "Come on!" Then once more he heard that wonderful song, and his heart yearned to find the singer. Flying toward the sound, leading the hunter, the bird flitted through the leaves, while its bright red top made it easy to follow. At last it lighted on a cedar tree and began hammering on a branch, making a noise like the fast beating of a small drum. Suddenly there was a gust of wind, and again the hunter heard that beautiful sound right above him.

Then he discovered that the song came from the dead branch that the woodpecker was tapping with his beak. He realized also that it was the wind which made the sound as it whistled through the holes the bird had drilled.

"*Kola,* friend," said the hunter, "let me take this branch home. You can make yourself another."

He took the branch, a hollow piece of wood full of woodpecker holes that was about the length of his forearm. He walked back to his village bringing no meat, but happy all the same.

In his tipi the young man tried to make the branch sing for him. He blew on it, he waved it around; no sound came. It made him sad, he wanted so much to hear that wonderful new sound. He purified himself in the sweat lodge and climbed to the top of a lonely hill. There, resting with his back against a large rock, he fasted, going without food or water for four days and nights, crying for a vision which would tell him how to make the branch sing. In the middle of the fourth night, *wagnuka,* the bird with the bright-red top, appeared, saying, "Watch me," turning himself into a man, showing the hunter how to make the branch sing, saying again and again: "Watch this, now." And in his dream the young man watched and observed very carefully.

When he awoke, he found a cedar tree. He broke off a branch and, working many hours, hollowed it out with a bowstring drill, just as he had seen the woodpecker do it in his dream. He whittled the branch into the shape of a bird with a long neck and an open beak. He painted the top of the bird's head with *washasha,* the sacred red color. He prayed. He smoked the branch up with incense of burning sage, cedar, and sweet grass. He fingered the holes as he had seen the man-bird do in his vision, meanwhile blowing softly into the mouthpiece. All at once there was the song, ghost-like and beautiful beyond words drifting all the way to the village, where the people were astounded and joyful to hear it. With the help of the wind and the woodpecker, the young man had brought them the first flute.

In the village lived an *itanchan*—the big chief. The *itanchan* had a daughter who was beautiful but also very proud, and convinced that there was no young man good enough for her. Many had come courting, but she had sent them all away. Now, the hunter who had made the flute decided that she was just the woman for him. Thinking of her he composed a special song, and one night, standing behind a tall tree, he played it on his *siyotanka* in hopes that it might have a charm to make her love him.

All at once the *winchinchala* heard it. She was sitting in her father's tipi, eating buffalo-hump meat and tongue, feeling good. She wanted to stay there, in the tipi by the fire, but her feet wanted to go outside. She pulled back, but the feet pulled forward, and the feet won. Her head said, "Go slow, go slow!" but the feet said, "Faster, faster!" She saw the young man standing in the moonlight; she heard the flute. Her head said, "Don't go to him; he's poor." Her feet said, "Go, run!" and again the feet prevailed.

So they stood face to face. The girl's head told her to be silent, but the feet told her to speak, and speak she did, saying: "*Koshkalaka,* young man, I am yours altogether." So they lay down together, the young man and the *winchinchala,* under one blanket.

Later she told him: "*Koshkalaka,* warrior, I like you. Let your parents send a gift to my father, the chief. No matter how small, it will be accepted. Let your father speak for you to my father. Do it soon! Do it now!"

And so the two fathers quickly agreed to the wishes of their children. The proud *winchinchala* became the hunter's wife, and he himself became a great chief. All the other young men had heard and seen. Soon they too began to whittle cedar branches into the shape of birds' heads with long necks and open beaks. The beautiful love music traveled from tribe to tribe, and made young girls' feet go where they shouldn't. And that's how the flute was brought to the people, thanks to the cedar, the woodpecker, and this young man, who shot no elk, but knew how to listen.

⌒ ⌒

"THE SERPENT OF THE SEA"
(from the Zuni)

"Let us abide with the ancients tonight!" exclaims the elder.
"Be it well," reply the listeners.

In the times of our forefathers there was a village under Thunder Mountain called Home of the Eagles. It is now in ruins: the roofs gone, the ladders decayed, the hearths cold. But when it was alive, it was the home of a beautiful maiden, the daughter of the priest-chief. Though beautiful, she had one strange trait: she could not endure the slightest speck of dust or dirt upon her clothes or person.

A sacred spring of water lay at the foot of the terrace on which the town stood. Now we call it the Pool of the Apaches, but then it was sacred to Kolowissi, the Serpent of the Sea. Washing her clothes and bathing herself over and over, the maiden spent almost all her time at this spring. The defilement of his waters, their contamination by the dirt of her apparel and the dun of her person, angered Kolowissi. He devised a plan to punish her.

When the maiden next came to the spring, she was startled to find a smiling baby boy gurgling and splashing in the water. Of course it was the Sea Serpent who, like the other gods, can assume any form at his pleasure. The girl looked all around—north, south, east, and west—but saw no trace of a person who might have left the beautiful child. "Whose can it be?" she wondered. "Only a cruel mother would leave her baby here to die!"

The maiden talked softly to the child, took him in her arms, and carried him up the hill to her house. There she brought him into her room, where she lived apart from her family because of her loathing of dust and dirt. As she played with him, laughing at his pranks and smiling into his face, he answered her in a baby fashion with coos and smiles of his own.

Meanwhile her younger sisters had prepared the evening meal and were waiting for her. "Where can she be?" they asked.

"Probably at the spring, as usual!" said their father. "Run down and call her."

But the youngest sister could not find her at the spring, so she came home and climbed to the maiden's private room at the top of the house. And there the maiden was, sitting on the floor and playing with the beautiful baby.

On hearing this the father was silent and thoughtful, for he knew that the waters of the spring were sacred. When the rest of the family started to climb the ladder to see the child, he called them back.

"Do you suppose any real mother would leave her baby in a spring?" he said. "This is not as simple as it seems." And since the maiden would not leave the child, they ate without her.

Upstairs the baby began to yawn. Growing drowsy herself, the girl put him on the bed and fell asleep beside him.

The maiden's sleep was real, the baby's a pretense. He lay quietly and began to lengthen, drawing himself out, extending longer and longer. Slowly the Serpent of the Sea appeared, like a nightmare come true. He was so huge that he had to coil himself round and round the room, filling it with scaly, gleaming circles. Placing his enormous head near the maiden's,

Kolowissi surrounded her with his coils and finally took his own tail into his mouth.

So the night passed. In the morning when breakfast was ready and the oldest sister had not come down, the others grew impatient.

"Now that she has child, nothing else matters to her," the old man said. "A baby is enough to absorb any woman's attention."

But the smallest sister climbed up to the room and called her. Receiving no answer, she pushed the door, first gently and then with all her might. She could not move it and began to be frightened. Running to the skyhole over the room where the others were sitting, she cried for help.

Everyone except the father rushed up, and pushing together, cracked the door just enough to catch a glimpse of the serpent's great scales. Then they screamed and ran back down.

The father, priest and sage that he was, told them quietly, "I expected as much. I thought it was impossible for a woman to be so foolish as to leave her child in a spring. But it's not impossible, it seems, for another woman to be so foolish as to take such a child to her bosom."

Climbing up to her room, he pushed against the door and called, "Oh Kolowissi, it is I who speak to you—I, your priest. I pray you, let my child come to me again, and I will make atonement for her errors. She is yours; but let her return to us once more."

Hearing this, the Serpent of the Sea began to loosen his coils. The whole building, the whole village, shook violently, and everyone trembled with fear.

At last the maiden awoke and cried piteously for help. As the coils unwound, she was able to rise. The great serpent bent the folds of his body nearest the doorway so that they formed an arch for her to pass under. She was half stunned by the din of the monster's scales, which rasped against one another like the scraping of flints under the feet of a rapid runner.

Once clear of the writhing mass, the maiden was away like a deer. Tumbling down the ladder and into the room below, she threw herself on her mother's breast.

But the priest remained, praying to the serpent. He ended with: "It shall be as I have said; she is yours!"

He and the two warrior-priests of the town called together all the other priests in sacred council. Performing the solemn rites, they prepared plumes, prayer wands, and offerings of treasure. After four days of ceremonies, the old priest called his daughter and told her that she must give these offerings, together with the most precious of them all, herself, to the Serpent of the Sea. She must renounce her people and her home and dwell in the house of Kolowissi in the Waters of the World.

"Your deeds tell me," said her father, "that this has been your desire. For you brought this fate on yourself by using the sacred water for profane purposes." The maiden wept and clung to her mother's neck. Then, shivering with terror, she left her childhood home. In the plaza they dressed her with earrings, bracelets, beads and other precious things. Amidst the lamentations of the people, they painted her cheeks with red spots as if for a dance. They made a road of sacred meal toward the distant spring known as the Doorway of the Serpent of the Sea. Four steps toward this spring they marked out sacred terraces on the ground at the west of the plaza. And when they finished the sacred road, the old priest, without one tear, told his daughter to walk out on it and call the serpent to come.

At once the door opened and the Serpent of the Sea descended from the maiden's room, where he had been waiting. Without using ladders, he lowered his head and breast down to the ground in great undulations. He placed his heavy head on the maiden's shoulder, and the priests said, "It is time."

Slowly, cowering beneath her burden, the maiden started toward the west. Whenever she staggered with fear and weariness and was about to wander from the path, the serpent gently pushed her onward and straightened her course.

They went toward the river trail and followed it, then crossed over the Mountain of the Red Paint, and still the serpent was not completely uncoiled from the maiden's room. Not until they were past the mountain did his tail emerge.

Suddenly Kolowissi drew himself together and began to assume a new shape. Before long his serpent form contracted and shortened until he lifted his head from the maiden's shoulder and stood up, a beautiful young man in sacred ceremonial dress! He slipped his serpent scales, now grown smaller, under his flowing mantle. In the snake's hoarse hiss he said: "Are you tired, girl?" She never replied, but plodded on with her eyes cast down.

In a gentler voice he said, "Are you weary, poor maiden?" rising taller, walking a little behind her, he wrapped his scales more closely in his blanket. He repeated in a still softer voice, "Are you weary, poor maiden?"

At first she dared not look around, though the voice sounded so changed, so kind. Yet she still felt the weight of the serpent's head on her shoulder, for she had become used to the heavy burden and could not tell that it had gone. At last, however, she turned and saw a splendid, brave young man, magnificently dressed.

"May I walk by your side?" he asked. "Why don't you speak?"

"I am filled with fear and shame," said she.

"Why? What do you fear?"

"I came away from my home with a terrifying creature, and he rested his head upon my shoulder, and even now I feel it there." She lifted her hand to the place where it had been, still fearing that she would find it.

"But I came all the way with you," said he, "and I saw no such creature."

She stopped and looked at him. "You came all the way? Then where has the serpent gone?"

He smiled and replied, "I know where he has gone."

"Ah, my friend, will he leave me alone now? Will he let me return to my people?"

"No, because he thinks too much of you."

"Where is he?"

"He is here," said the youth, smiling and placing his hand on his heart. "I am he."

"I don't believe it!" cried the maiden.

He drew the shriveled serpent scales out from under his mantle. "I am he, and I love you, beautiful maiden! Won't you come and stay with me? We will live and love one another not just now, but forever, in all the Waters of the World."

And as they journeyed on, the maiden quite forgot her sadness, and soon she forgot her home too. She followed her husband into the Doorway of the Serpent of the Sea and lived with him ever after.

Helpful Hints for Incorporating Native American Poetry and Folklore into a Modern Wedding Ceremony:

YOU may find poems that you would like to include as part of your wedding ceremony. The poems could be read before or during the wedding ceremony. Certainly the last two poems (on pages 29–30) quoted have their refreshing charms.

It may be nice to include some poetry at the end of the ceremony program, even if it is not read during the service. Some brides and grooms may choose to write their own vows, and traditional poetry could certainly be incorporated into the vows, or at least serve as an inspiration.

Some couples may choose to recite the vows or poetry in the original language, and then read the English translation. This would definitely add a special touch to the ceremony by bringing a part of ancient cultural tradition into the modern wedding.

These poems are only a sampling of poems that have appeared in collections of Indian prose and poetry. The Barnes book[2] is available in the New York Public Library, and may be available at libraries throughout the country. The Levitas, Vivelo, and Vivelo book can be found in the reference library of the George Gustav Heye Center, National Museum of the American Indian in New York City. The Heye Center has several collections of poems available only for reference work and also different collections of poems for sale in the bookstore.

Books of Indian poetry are available in most major bookstores around the country, and there should be a selection of poems in libraries at universities and in any academic or public library system.

The two folk tales included in this book are both charming love stories. The first, "The Legend of the Flute," would be a delightful piece to read before the ceremony begins. A couple may choose to have a flutist perform some traditional music right after the story is read to tie it in with the proceedings.

The second folk tale, "The Serpent of the Sea," is a variation of the Beauty and the Beast story, and as it ends with a happy marriage, may also be good choice for reading, either at the wedding ceremony itself, or earlier at a rehearsal dinner or even a family gathering that celebrates the couple's engagement.

There are several collections of Native American folklore and legends available at libraries and bookstores. Brides and grooms may want to do a little research to find stories from a particular tribe or region. Beautiful poetry and traditional love stories would not only set a Native American-inspired ceremony apart from the usual ones, but would also give brides and grooms a chance to share the richness of their cultural heritage with guests.

NOTES

1. From: *The Sky Clears: North American Indian Poetry*, by A. Grove Day, University of Nebraska Press, Lincoln, 1951.
2. *American Indian Love Lyrics and Other Verse*, selected by Nellie Barnes, The Macmillan Company, New York, 1925.
3. *American Indian Prose and Poetry*, edited and introduced by Gloria Levitas, Frank Robert Vivelo, Jacqueline J. Vivelo, G.P. Putnam's Sons, New York. The poem "I Sit Here Thinking of Her" comes from Frances Densmore's collection, *Poems From Sioux and Chippewa Songs*, and "I Am Arrayed Like the Roses" comes from Densmore's collection, *Chippewa Music*.
4. *American Indian Poetry: An Anthology of Songs and Chants*, edited by George W. Cronyn, Liveright Publishing Corp., New York, 1934, Copyright renewed by George W. Cronyn, 1962.
5. *American Indian Myths and Legends,* selected and edited by Richard Erdoes and Alfonso Ortiz, Pantheon Books, New York, 1984.

Introduction to Tribal Wedding Customs

Every tribe—eastern, western, southern or northern—forbids incest, and violation of the proscription was punishable by death. Therefore, obviously, a parent and child, or sisters and brothers, could not marry. Beyond that, there were great variations from tribe to tribe about what constituted incest. Some tribes looked very favorably upon marriages between some first cousins. However, all the tribes forbade marriages between members of the same clan; a clan was regarded as a family, even if, to the larger, white society, a clan didn't seem to be composed of only close relatives. The complexities of clan membership

are enormous. To this day, Indians respect relationships between people in the same clan, and even if
the members of a clan are not second or third cousins,
a marriage between them is considered incestuous,
and therefore unacceptable.

It is difficult for anyone but an expert on Indian
cultures to understand clan rules and regulations,
which have virtually nothing in common with the
laws in force regarding incest or the wedding customs
of the larger society in the United States. Otherwise,
the wedding traditions and rites of Native Americans,
though they may differ from tribe to tribe in many
ways, are easy to understand and rather fascinating
as well.

The Hopis and Navajos, both tribes in the southwest, primarily Arizona and New Mexico, have many
principles in common, though they differ in specific
traditions about marriages. Both used to require that a
groom pay a bride price, and the bride's family also
paid tribute to the groom's family with gifts of equal
and sometimes even greater value. Most tribes have
shared that custom; in some tribes, the exchange of
gifts constituted the entire wedding ceremony. And
sometimes the contract was even simpler than that.

One Teton Sioux man named Fools Crow remembered July 4, 1916 as his surprise engagement and
wedding day.[1] A very active individual who regularly
competed as a jockey, racer and dancer, he was

working with a few racehorses and a relay team in Kyle, South Dakota. At dinner time, he was sitting with his family when a girl named Fannie, the youngest daughter of friends of his family, came to his camp. She told him that her family wanted to talk with him. So he left his dinner and followed her, unable to guess the reason for the invitation.

At her camp, her parents served him dinner. They also told him that Fannie had fallen in love and wanted to marry him, and her parents approved. Fools Crow didn't know what to say at first, but then replied that he would discuss the matter with his father. His father told him that he and Fannie's parents had already decided it was a very good idea.

Fools Crow thought it over, went back to get Fannie and a few of her possessions, and moved them to his camp. "As simply as that we were wed," he recounted to Thomas E. Mails in the book.[1] "I feel it was one of the best decisions of my life, for we had a wonderful marriage . . ."

If the two families made any deal about property, Fools Crow never mentioned it. Quite possibly, the parents did make arrangements that were more complicated than he mentioned, but if so, Fannie's and his parents took care of them, and Fools Crow seems never to have given them a second thought.

For some tribes, the arrangements were painstakingly worked out in steps that took a lot of time,

primarily because they concerned property, possessions and prestige. Both the Hopis and Navajos, as
only two examples, are matrilineal tribes, meaning
that their property is passed down by the women.
There are other tribes which are patrilineal. The dis-
tinction has been very important, particularly when
it involves divorce—a common occurrence in many
tribes. In matrilineal tribes, the women retain all the
property, and the children always stay with the
mother or her family. Not only among the Hopis and
Navajos, but in most tribes, the children of a divorced
couple, or even of a widowed husband, remain with
the mother's family.

Luckily, non-Indians don't need to understand the
elaborate rules and regulations of family and clan relationships within tribes to enjoy the traditions of Native
American weddings.

NOTE

1. *Fools Crow*, by Thomas E. Mails, University of Nebraska Press,
   Lincoln, Nebraska, 1979. This book was based on interviews
   with Fools Crow in the 1970s.

3
Tribal Wedding Customs — The Hopi

The Hopi of Arizona celebrate all types of milestones in life with very specific rites symbolizing the continuity of life. When couples were in the courting stage, if a Hopi boy wanted a girl to become his bride, he made a bundle for her—clothing and fine white buckskin moccasins—and left them on her doorstep. If she accepted them, she accepted him, too.[1] A wedding involves both blood relatives and members of the family related by affinity or close relationships. All the relatives have certain tasks they're obliged to perform. Some require a great deal of time and effort. A Hopi wedding may take such a long time to prepare for that the couple may already have several children by the time the parents are married; they include the children in the wedding ceremony. It's so common for the couple to have children at their wedding that the children, too, dress in a prescribed fashion for the celebration.

A Hopi wedding is a serious occasion for the relatives of the bride and groom. The bride is not supposed to smile when she wears the robes woven for her by the groom's uncles. In the Hopi tradition, the male relatives of the bridegroom create the bride's robes for her wedding day. Hopi men are the weavers. The rites of the wedding are supposed to be a rehearsal for, or an enactment of, the rest of the bride's life, even to the detail of a robe she carries for a later ceremony—her burial. (In some tribes, the bride is expected to keep her wedding dress for her burial gown, but Hopi brides get separate garments for their weddings and funerals.)

Even though a couple is not technically married until the wedding day, everyone treats the children as legitimate offspring and fully deserving members of the family. Their relatives keep them away from sunlight until they are about three weeks old, and then they are taken out to see the sun rise at dawn. At that time, the child's life officially dawns, and he or she receives a name. In the days before a Hopi wedding takes place, the bride spends time, most sources say four days, grinding corn. Some sources say she does it in her mother-in-law's house, and some simply say she does the grinding in the presence of other female relatives, who grind corn with her. Corn is a very significant part of the Hopi Indians' lives, and for that matter historically extremely important for most tribes. The Hopis attach significance to blue corn, for example. Traditional Hopi belief teaches that blue corn plays a part in their origins. Upon arriving in this world, Hopis were offered corn of various colors, and their choice determined their destiny. They chose the short, blue ear of corn; though it signified that their lives would be difficult, it also meant they would learn to survive and outlive all other people on this planet.

While the bride grinds corn inside the house, various relatives wage a battle outdoors. No one gets hurt, but the fight makes a mess. To get the fight started, the groom's paternal aunts arrive at his house with buckets of mud. They're met by his maternal aunts, who also have buckets of mud. The bride's maternal and paternal aunts arrive, too, similarly armed. The aunts throw the mud at each other. (Notice it's the aunts, not the uncles, in this matrilineal tribe.) One group insults the groom, while the other group insults the bride. According to one source, the maternal aunts may capture the groom's father, cut his hair, and thereby enact a mock scalping. At the end of the fight, everyone is exhausted, filthy, and hungry. But everyone joins together to enjoy a feast, and the bride and groom are supposed to live happily ever after. (Jill McManus, a jazz pianist and writer who lives in New York City, and who has spent a great deal of time with the Hopis in Arizona and has even composed and recorded a highly praised jazz recording, "The Sounds of Hopi," says the mud slinging supposedly allows the relatives to vent their aggressions and hostilities before the wedding and to exorcise any demons that might cast a pall over the couple's marriage.)

The day after the mud fight, the wedding takes place. The bride, followed by the groom carrying a side of mutton (a popular meat in many Hopi feasts and ceremonies), along with the groom's relatives, form a procession that walks to the bride's mother's house. There everyone celebrates the marriage with a feast.

In a very beautiful book about the Hopis, called *Hopi*, by Susanne and Jake Page, photographs show a relative arranging a groom's mother's hair for the wedding day.[2] The bride of this couple already has a daughter; the child wears white deerskin moccasins and leggings—traditional wedding clothes for a child— and she has her hair styled by relatives. All the people participating in the wedding have their faces dusted with cornmeal, which is considered sacred.

In this case, the wedding took place at the home of the bride's in-laws. The bride and her daughter both wore white cotton robes woven by the groom's uncles. (Cotton dresses have long been traditional among the Hopi, while other tribes wore clothes of other fabrics, particularly animal skins.) The bride's second robe for her burial is of cotton, too; she carries it rolled up in a mat woven of reeds. The wedding celebration includes spruce boughs and prayer feathers worked together as an offering to the spirits.

In some ways it might have appeared to white settlers, when they first encountered Indian societies, that Indians had common law marriages, since they weren't blessed by a church or recorded by any government. And women seemed to be subservient to their husbands. But negotiations for the bride prices, which always took place when the Indians lived only under their own tribal governments, not only made the wedding arrangements serious business, but symbolized the serious attitude of Native Americans toward their family structures. Particularly in matrilineal tribes such as the Hopi, Navajo, Cherokee, and Iroquois, among others—tribes in which the property was passed down by the women, not the men— women weren't chattel at all. The men had more to lose than the women when couples divorced.

In the matrilineal society of many Indian tribes, the bride always had important rights over her status and future. If she and her husband did not get along, they could divorce at any time. All the wife had to do was place his belongings outside the house where they lived. The husband, on his side, could break up the marriage simply by leaving the house and never returning. If there were children, they stayed with the mother and her family. No one asked questions about who had the rights to the children and the property; all was the wife's.

Helpful Hints for Bringing Old Hopi Traditions into a Modern Wedding:

IF the bride already has a daughter, or if a bride is inviting a young girl to act as the flower girl, the bride may want to dress her in a white cotton gown and white doeskin moccasins with leggings to wear for the ceremony. For other ideas about wedding party dresses, see the chapter about *Fashions.*

Since corn is of such special significance to the Hopi, as well as to most Indian tribes, the wedding dinner should include at least one very special corn-based dish. See the chapter about *Food* for ideas and menus for wedding feasts.

Indian females wear their hair in prescribed ways at different times of their lives. See the chapter about *Fashions.* The bride or any women in the bridal party may want to adapt any of the traditional hairstyles for the wedding.

NOTES

1. *The World of the American Indian*, National Geographic Society, Washington, D.C. 1993.
2. *Hopi*, by Susanne and Jake Page, Abradale Press, Harry N. Abrams, Inc., New York, 1992.

4

TRIBAL WEDDING
CUSTOMS —
THE NAVAJO

Susanne Page, who first began photographing the Navajo in Arizona and New Mexico in the 1960s, became especially involved in the life of one little Navajo girl and her family. When the girl was about 18 years old, she decided to get married and invited Susanne to attend the ceremony and take photographs. The bride sent out invitations—not usually a practice in a Navajo wedding.

But wherever traditional weddings still take place, they are mixed with the customs of the larger, American society. Traditional Indian weddings—rare events now—take place only in Indian communities that have not had their cultures eradicated or at least extremely diluted by the larger society. It may be startling to realize that the United States granted citizenship to Native Americans only as recently as 1924. Previously their legal status was "wards of the state." Even so, Indians have been marrying according to the traditions of the Christian churches and other sanctioned officiators for much longer than that.

Susanne arrived at the bride's house in Rough Rock, Arizona, the bride's "hometown," at one o'clock, the hour for which the wedding ceremony was scheduled. From there, Susanne went to a hogan a distance up a hill from the house, where the wedding would actually take place. To get there, she walked in the direction of Black Mesa, a high formation of rock about 60 by 30 miles wide, a major feature of the land in northeastern Arizona. The hogan was decorated with balloons. Otherwise it gave no hint of the coming ceremony. The bride didn't appear; she was busy getting dressed.

The ceremony didn't actually start for another three hours. Unlike Susanne, the other guests had expected the delay, and they began to trickle into the hogan during the afternoon. The groom's family arrived from the escarpment, Black Mesa, which, on its distant southern edge, is home to Hopi villages. Susanne discovered the wedding was scheduled to take place so late in the day because Navajo tradition dictates that the sun must reach a particular position in the western sky—specifically, at sundown—before the ceremony could start.

Inside the hogan, the groom headed south, following the path of the sun, walking left, and sat on the floor. His family sat by him to the north. One of the bride's uncles, a medicine man, together with a small procession of people, went to the hogan with a cup of water in hand. Another uncle and the bride's mother carried food. The bride walked with them, wearing her "moccasins, deerskin leggings, a white satin skirt and a blouse, bedecked in what appeared to be all the family's turquoise jewelry—bracelets, squash blossom necklaces," writes Susanne Page in her book, *Navajo*.[1] The bride also wore a colorful shawl that she had bought for the occasion. Squash blossom necklaces are traditional fertility symbols among the Hopi and other tribes.

"She carried a shallow basket woven of yucca in which there was a layer of cornmeal mush," Susanne noted, too.[1] When the procession neared the hogan, the bride's mother handed Susanne a tray of food and told her to lead the procession into the hogan. About 50 people had gathered there in the very warm room.

The bride sat on the groom's right; her family sat on her right. She set the basket with the cornmeal mush on the floor in front of the group. The guests had already put their gifts of food for the wedding feast and their private gifts for the couple on the floor, too.

The medicine man, the bride's uncle, kneeled in front of the couple and directed them to wash their hands in the cup of water he had brought. Then he took corn pollen from a pouch and made lines across the mush in the basket. The lines pointed in four directions according to tradition. Some lines were drawn in white cornmeal, and some in yellow cornmeal.

Speaking the Navajo language as he told the couple about the responsibilities of marriage, he changed the position of the pollen basket. Susanne later learned that the movement was supposed to turn the bride and groom's minds toward each other. The medicine man directed the couple to eat some of the pollen.

Susanne was then surprised to learn she was supposed to lead the couple in reciting the "white man's vows." Conjuring up wedding ceremony vows from memory, she squatted down, asked the couple to hold hands, and guided them. And the couple was married. Then the ceremony turned even more festive, as everyone dined, while the couple opened their presents and made a fuss about how wonderful the wedding and the presents were. One of the bride's sisters made her first appearance at the wedding at this time; she wore such an elaborate hairdo that Susanne thought it looked like "a Burmese temple."[1]

Susanne ended her account by saying the wedding was the last in a variety of ceremonies or rites that took place in a Navajo girl's life, such as the celebrations at her birth and for the advent of puberty.

Susanne had not witnessed the preliminaries to this wedding. In this case, because it was a modern marriage, the couple's families probably paid nothing vaguely resembling a bride price, and certainly they wouldn't have negotiated about an exchange of horses or household goods in the old-fashioned way. For those negotiations, when Navajos lived only by their ancient customs, the two families used to sit down together and negotiate the price. Horses and other such practical items often served as the price, and also as a symbolic, serious merging of the couple's family assets.

In the Navajo tribe, the groom's payment was of major importance. It was shameful for a Navajo bride to marry without receiving a bride price. The bride's family probably would have paid at least as great a tribute. That was the custom in most Native American tribes. It was the duty and privilege of the bride's family to hold its head high, as it were, and assert equality for the bride and groom. White colonists may have originally thought that payment for a bride made her seem like a prostitute or a piece of property, but ironically in the view of the Navajos, a woman who married without receiving a bride price was akin to a prostitute. To be paid for was honorable. When the price was right, the marriage got off to a bright start.

The price didn't guarantee that the marriage would last. But the price did guarantee that the women had respectable standing in the tribe and primary rights to the couple's property and children.

Helpful Hints for Bringing Old Navajo Traditions into a Modern Wedding:

To add a touch of the earthiness of traditions thousands of years old among the Navajo, a modern bride and groom can elect to have a small, very tightly woven, yucca basket or plate of cornmeal mush, with white and yellow cornmeal lines crossing it and depicting the four directions, at the altar. The Franciscan Brothers published a book, *An Ethnology Dictionary of the Navajo Language*,[2] explaining the cornmeal-in-a-basket rite fully.

The basket, which was usually woven of yucca braid, had to be new. In the traditional marriage ceremony, a relative of the bride drew lines in the cornmeal mush, with white and yellow cornmeal, and then drew a circle with yellow cornmeal around the whole, beginning and ending at the line with its end pointing to the east. After the hand washing ceremony of the bride and groom, the relative in charge of the basket turned it to have the east end of the line facing the couple. The bridegroom took a pinch of the cornmeal mush with his fingers, ate it, and then the bride dipped her fingers in at the same place and took a pinch to eat, too. The bride and groom did the same thing at the end of each line in the mush in the basket. That rite actually concluded the Navajo wedding ceremony.

Since it was impossible for the couple to eat all the cornmeal mush, they passed it around to all the guests. Whoever ate the last bit of the cornmeal won possession of the basket. Sometimes the basket was simply given to the bride's mother, who was not present at the wedding in the old days; she and her son-in-law weren't supposed to look at each other, according to a tradition now long gone. Or sometimes the basket went to the groom's family, and the person who drove up the horses which were part of the bride gift consumed the last portion of the cornmeal. In traditional Navajo weddings, the conclusion of the basket ceremony signaled the start of the feast.

NOTES

1. *Navajo*, by Susanne and Jake Page, Harry N. Abrams Publishers, Inc., New York, 1995.
2. *An Ethnology Dictionary of the Navajo Language*, by the Franciscan Brothers, Saint Michaels, Arizona, 1910.

5

TRIBAL WEDDING CUSTOMS—THE STORY OF AN EASTERN CHEROKEE BRIDE AND A MINNESOTA SIOUX BRIDEGROOM

Nikoa, a bride-to-be in 1999, comes from the matrilineal Eastern Cherokee in North Carolina. She belongs to her mother's clan, one of seven clans in her tribe. When she marries her fiancé, a Sioux Indian from Minnesota, he will automatically become a member of her clan. And she will become a member of his clan automatically. Nobody else in his or her family becomes members of the other person's clan. So the bridegroom's brother could marry the bride's sister. But neither Nikoa nor her fiancé could marry anyone from their own clans. That would be incestuous. In the old days, Nikoa would have had to marry someone from her own tribe—but not her clan. In those days, Indians didn't leave their reservations or, before the days of the reserves, their community groups. "We wouldn't have even met someone from another tribe," Nikoa explains.

Though she was raised as a Christian, she doesn't go to church. Her fiancé believes in the traditional religion of the Sioux. So the couple decided to get married in a traditional Sioux wedding ceremony in Minnehaha County, on the Shakopee reserve, about 30 minutes from Minneapolis, Minnesota. The bride-to-be didn't know what the ceremony would consist of, but she was going to wear the traditional clothes, whatever they were.

The couple will later decide which clan to register their children in. They could be either Cherokee or Sioux; the couple will base their decision upon land benefits and federally-provided health care benefits, whatever will be most profitable for the child.

Though no one in the bride-to-be's family has been married in a traditional Eastern Cherokee wedding ceremony, Nikoa knows what it used to consist of.

A wedding vase was filled with a liquid important to the tribe. The vase had two spigots. The groom drank from one spigot, and the bride from the other.[1] A blanket was tied around the couple. "Nobody ever had a divorce back then," Nikoa says, "and if someone wanted to get divorced and married again, the blanket was untied and put away." The husband or wife or both were free to marry other people. "The blanket was like the wedding band," says Nikoa, an employee at the American Indian Community House in New York City.

⟳ ⟳

Myths of the Cherokee and Sacred Formulas of the Cherokees,[2] by James Mooney tells of the ways that Cherokee marriages were arranged. Among nearly all the tribes, with the exception of the Pueblo, the hopeful bridegroom first received the consent of the woman he wanted to marry. Then he gave presents to her parents as a kind of compensation for the loss of their daughter. The gift giving formalized the agreement between the man and woman. But if the parents felt the gifts were insufficient, they could refuse them, and the marriage didn't take place. So the hopeful suitor usually asked a friend or the brother of the girl to act as a go-between to settle the bride price with the parents.

Another source, *Weaving New Worlds: Southeastern Cherokee Women and Their Basketry,* by Sarah H. Hill,[3] recounts the custom of the suitor, having received permission to marry a woman, he lay a present of wood at the door of his beloved's house. She signaled her acceptance by making a fire with the wood and offering him food to eat. The trade confirmed the marriage. Then the man's family brought a great amount of wood to the woman, and her relatives prepared a feast for both sides of the family.

An observer of the Eastern Cherokees and their wedding customs in about the year 1700 noticed that a young man always went himself or sent a go-between to a girl's family to arrange a match. Elder brothers often acted as the go-betweens for both young women and hopeful suitors. The parents answered that they would think about requests for their daughters as brides, then discussed the matter with all their relatives. Even the tribe's leader might give his opinion. If they approved, and if the young woman accepted the match, the suitor paid a bride price to her parents. (The better looking the girl, the higher the price.) In any case, the marriage took place only if the bride-to-be approved of it. The Indians never gave their young women in marriage against their will.

Helpful Hints for Bringing Old Cherokee Traditions into a Modern Wedding:

A couple can drink wine or any liquid that they choose out of the same cup or glass (an ornate chalice would be very appropriate) during a wedding ceremony.

Even more picturesque, and easy for all the guests to see, a couple can choose a blanket, perhaps an authentic Native American blanket or shawl, to wrap around themselves during the ceremony or just after the wedding officiator says that the groom and bride may kiss as husband and wife. The officiator or a member of the wedding party can tie a knot in the garment, and then it can be folded and left that way for the couple to keep.

NOTES

1. See chapter 11 on *Fashions* for a mention of the small Hopi and Santa Clara wedding jugs (silver pottery) in the section: "Books on Indian Jewelry." These miniature sculptures are available for sale.
2. *Myths of the Cherokee and Sacred Formulas of the Cherokees*, by James Mooney, reprinted by Charles and Randy Elder, Nashville, Tennessee, 1982.
3. *Weaving New Worlds: Southeastern Cherokee Women and Their Basketry*, by Sarah H. Hill, published by The University of North Carolina Press, Chapel Hill, N.C., and London, 1997.

6

TRIBAL WEDDING CUSTOMS — THE IROQUOIS

Among the tribes that especially like to protect their privacy are the Iroquois, who are leery of being used and commercialized. They do not invite outsiders, as a general rule, to observe the ways they conduct their daily lives or their ceremonies and celebrations. Nevertheless a great deal, much of it admiring, has been written about their history, including their family, clan, and tribal structure, from the point of view of non-Indian observers.

The Iroquois have always been a matrilineal society to such a degree that outside observers, from the early settlers in North America to contemporary scholars, have seemed to take a kind of pity on the men. Men were always subject to the rule of the women. Iroquois men were also very respectful of all women, both white and Indian women, observers said.

The Iroquois absolutely prohibited marriages between men and women of the same clan, and to this day they stick to this tradition. Most marriages were historically monogamous. Fathers never involved themselves in marriage arrangements for their children. That was woman's work—and done strictly under women's authority.

When a mother thought her son was ready to get married, she looked around for a suitable girl, then negotiated the bride price with the girl's mother. Sometimes the mothers consulted relatives, but the ultimate decision belonged to the mothers, and not to the children. Sometimes the couple didn't even know about the agreement and arrangements until they were told that the marriage was in the immediate offing. The children rarely objected. Their parents had taught them to be completely obedient, or else they, both the girls and the boys, could be disowned. Being disowned could be incredibly costly, especially to the women, who essentially inherited everything they owned from their mothers. Their mothers, not their fathers, owned everything.

On rare occasions, when a girl had been ready for marriage for quite a while and still had not attracted a suitor, the mother of the girl might initiate a marriage.

The wedding ceremony was simple. On the day after a marriage was announced, the bride, accompanied by her mother or maternal grandmother, went to the house of the groom's maternal grandmother and gave her some wedding cakes carried in a basket. The number of cakes varied, according to some sources, from five or six to as many as 24. It depended upon how big the groom's family was. The offering of the cakes proved that the young woman's family approved of the marriage.

The mother of the groom had to accept the cakes, unless she had some very valid objection. If she did reject them, then she left the cakes untouched on the doorstep. Eventually the family of the young woman, who would have become a bride, took the cakes away—and felt humiliated.

But if the marriage went through, relatives and friends of the groom ate the cakes and replaced them in the empty basket with meat. They returned the basket to the girl's family, who ate the meat with their relatives. Then the two families met, and important men in the tribes made speeches, expressed happiness at the marriage, and gave the newlyweds advice about married life.

The couple had to follow many rules and go through a succession of rituals, and not all of them are well-known or have been confirmed outside of Iroquois society. A young man may have moved into his wife's family's house for a while, perhaps two years, and hunted and fished under the authority of his mother-in-law. He always offered her at least a portion, and sometimes all, of what he had caught. All the customs about marriage revolved around the lifestyle and survival tactics of the Iroquois.

Anyone interested in studying them can find materials in the reference library of the National Museum of the American Indian in New York City. One good book about the lifestyle of the Iroquois is *Iroquois Women: An Anthology*.[1]

Helpful Hints for Bringing Old Iroquois Traditions into a Modern Wedding:

JUST before the wedding ceremony takes place, or just after the vows are exchanged, or, probably most conveniently for all concerned, at the start of the wedding reception, waiters can serve, to both the bride's and groom's relatives and guests simultaneously, fancy cakes, some perhaps sweet cornbread cakes, and others small meat cakes, that can be easily eaten as canapés.

Since there's nothing that can be significantly construed as an Iroquois or any type of Indian tradition about serving such finger foods at the start of a wedding dinner, the hosts may want to print little messages on accompanying napkins or in the program, saying the cornbread cake and meat snacks were inspired by an old Iroquois tradition.

NOTE

1. *Iroquois Women: An Anthology*, edited by Wm. Guy Spittal, Iroqrafts, Ltd., Iroquois Publications, Ontario, Canada, 1990, 1996.

7
TRIBAL WEDDING CUSTOMS — LAKOTA — OGLALA SIOUX

The courtship and wedding traditions of the Oglala Sioux fascinated the white settlers arriving in Indian lands. Sometimes the Indian men kidnapped the Indian women or captured women from outside their tribe. The men also devised more peaceful alternatives for getting to the altar.

Sometimes a man dressed up in his best costume, painted his face in bright colors, and wore a courting robe. Then he walked back and forth in front of the door of the tipi where the woman he wanted to marry lived. She peered out, then came outside to watch him. He kept walking to and fro, inching closer to her, until he could touch her. For a moment, she might seem to struggle to get free. But then she calmed down. He took off his courting robe and wrapped it around the two of them. They stood together, looking out at the world, signaling that other men should stay away from the woman. She was no longer available— at least for the time being. The woman's family invited the man to sit with them, placing him beside the woman. If she smiled at him, she signaled that she was willing to accept him. But if she turned her back on him, she rejected him. If she accepted him, she gave him a drink of water and invited him to come back another time. When he returned, she offered him food that she had cooked. And if she decided she wanted to be his wife, she made a present of a pair of moccasins, which she decorated herself. If he wanted to marry her, he put the moccasins on right away. Then the couple was formally engaged.

The man's eldest, closest relative visited the woman's family and negotiated a bride price, usually six buffalo skins or their equal in value. A very hard working and pleasant woman might fetch an even higher price. Negotiations could take place over a period of several meetings, complete with feasts for the couple and invited guests, both family and friends.

The couple developed a more intimate relationship with each other when the young man sat near her tipi during the evenings and played the flute music that

Indians considered to be so seductive. The woman went to meet him. To support her, her girlfriends built little fires with cottonwood tree twigs as a symbolic way of chasing away disagreeable spirits that could cause arguments.

The bride's dowry usually consisted of a tipi, a pair of robes, a bone awl and sinew thread for the bride to use in sewing skins, a cooking utensil, an ax, and a knife. The tipi was especially important. It gave the young couple complete authority over their lives together. The couple might have a wedding before the bride offered her dowry, but the dowry had to be paid before the couple could be considered properly married.

For the wedding, the bride needed a dress of soft, tanned deer or antelope skin, with the bodice decorated with the teeth of dogs, and leggings reaching from the knee to the ankle, and made of soft, tanned skins, and decorated with porcupine quills and feathers arranged in prescribed designs, and moccasins of soft tanned skins for the uppers and rawhide soles decorated with porcupine quills or brightly painted designs. She parted her hair in the middle, combed it with a porcupine tail, oiled it with animal fat, and braided it into two or three sections. The braids hung down her back until she was married, and then she wore them hanging down in front of her shoulders.

If she had been treated to a puberty ceremony (see the next chapter about that ritual which all Indian tribes celebrated) she painted a red stripe along the part in her hair. And if she had also been through another ceremony, called the adoption ceremony, she wore another red stripe painted across her forehead. If she had participated in some sacred ceremony, she could have her hands painted red. If she was mourning someone, she could paint her face black.

When she was dressed and decorated in these ways, her fiancé brought the bride price to her tipi. Usually he arrived with his family and friends, with the women carrying the food for the feast. The bride and her family and friends also prepared feast food. As soon as the bride price was delivered, the bride took the man by the right hand, led him through the door of her tipi, and seated him in a place of honor, at the rear, opposite the door. She put a pair of moccasins on his feet, then sat in the woman's place in the tipi, at the right side of the fireplace in the center of the tipi. That constituted the wedding ceremony.

If the bride didn't have her own tipi and welcomed him to the place where she lived, the bride and groom were considered married, but they weren't counted as a family in the tribe's census. They had to behave in certain socially acceptable ways with her family, paying special deference to her relatives, until they had a tipi of their own. If they had a child while living in someone else's tipi, the child technically belonged to the tipi's owner. So the man and woman usually hurried to erect their own tipi as soon as they possibly could. The tipi always belonged to the wife.

When the couple had their own tipi, the man could take charge of the marriages of his wife's younger sisters. He might even marry the sisters, and he could approve or disapprove of their marrying other men. If he had more than one wife, he needed a tipi for each of them. But all the tipis counted as only one family unit. The first wife was always the predominant wife in the family.

Other protocols existed for families in which a man had more than one wife, but none of the subordinate wives had full-blown wedding ceremonies, except for a feast. Women captured from other tribes didn't even have a feast in honor of their marriages. They were considered married when they had learned to speak the Sioux language well. And the judges of their proficiency were Sioux women. Most marriages were monogamous, however, since there weren't usually enough women to provide more than one wife for each man. Furthermore the men discovered they could live in greater peace and harmony with one woman than with two or more.

Though the men had quite a lot of authority over women and possessed some hereditary birthrights, the tribe was essentially matrilineal about possessions. They raised boys and girls together, whether the parents became divorced or not. After a boy reached puberty, he came under the authority of his father or his father's relatives. Until the daughters married, they stayed with their mothers. Family relationships were very complex. All kinds of rights and privileges depended upon the order of the birth of children.

From a very early age, little girls were prepared for their roles as adults. Sioux girls knew they were expected to grow up to be mothers and raise their families skillfully. And they were supposed to value hard work and remain faithful to their husbands. (The usual causes of divorce were laziness and infidelity, and men divorced their wives by beating a drum at a public event and inviting other men to take the women.)

From the moment girls went through their first menstrual periods, they studied the arts of quill embroidery and moccasin-making. The girls may have already learned those skills before, but from that time on, they studied harder and worked more diligently. They had to learn quill and bead work, hide tanning, and excellent cooking techniques to prepare themselves to be good wives. Parents loved daughters who helped with household chores and took care of younger children.

So girls kept track of their achievements, putting colored dots on their scraping tools to record the number of tanned robes and tipis they made. The

Sioux held contests at which the young women exhibited their handiwork. Highly valued were cradles; beautiful cradles brought fame and fortune to their makers. "A cradle was equal in value to one horse."[1]

Girls were taught to say nothing to young men who came courting until the girls found the right man to marry. Promiscuous women were considered crazy. Older women counseled young women about sex, and the lessons were enhanced by various social rituals. One was called a Buffalo Ceremony and another was the Ball-throwing Rite, "at which a shaman, enlisting the aid of the supernaturals, officiated."[1] Everyone attended. These ceremonies were tantamount to social debuts.

Parents sometimes required their daughters to wear chastity belts. Young girls were probably wearing their chastity belts when suitors arrived in their best clothes and enveloped the women in blankets in front of their families' tipis, in full view of all the neighbors.

Young men had to strive to make themselves attractive and conquer competitors for the women of their choice. The men brushed their hair, plucked their beards, used perfumed grease, wore finely tanned robes, carefully quilled moccasins, and white shell earrings.[1] And some men were simply more charming than others. Also, they were expected to use love potions and medicines to increase their sex drive, and they studied playing cedar flutes made by shamans, who also composed romantic music.

Some flute players were so talented they could entice women to follow them and elope. When an elopement seemed to be in the offing, the parents of the young couple usually had the foresight to exchange their bride price gifts ahead of time.

Helpful Hints for Bringing Old Oglala Sioux Traditions into a Modern Wedding:

As it is with all weddings, the food can be a great center of attraction. See the chapter on *Food* for ideas about what to serve. For private gifts, the bride and groom can give each other authentic Indian moccasins made of soft animal skins sporting authentic Oglala Sioux designs.

At a party prior to the wedding, a man can use a robe to wrap around himself and his bride while they formally announce their engagement to friends.

NOTE

The information here about Oglala Sioux customs comes from the book, *Lakota Society*, by James R. Walker, edited by Raymond J. DeMallie, and published by the University of Nebraska Press, Lincoln, Nebraska, and London, 1982, in cooperation with the Colorado Historical Society. The information is corroborated in the book connoted by footnote 1: *The Sioux: Life and Customs of a Warrior Society*, by Royal B. Hassrick, University of Oklahoma Press, Norman, Oklahoma, and London, 1964.

8

CELEBRATIONS OF PUBERTY

When young Indian boys and girls, but especially girls, became adolescents, all the tribes staged elaborate celebrations. So important was this milestone for girls that, to this day, tribes which have not been assimilated or lost their traditions completely still celebrate. For the girls, the rites of puberty began immediately when they started to menstruate. Rites and feasts which introduced them to womanhood often went on for at least four days, and sometimes for a whole month. The celebrations were part-primitive superstition and part-Sweet Sixteen party, like many parties in cultures celebrating the coming of age of an adolescent.

Cubans celebrate when a girl turns fifteen. In the Jewish religion, when the children turn thirteen, the *bar mitzvah* marks the day when a boy becomes a man, and the *bat mitzvah* is the milestone for girls. Wealthy, society girls become debutantes at age eighteen; their parents present them at elegant parties as the latest season's eligible brides-to-be. In the cultures of all the American Indian tribes, the start of menstruation was considered such a major rite of passage that adolescent girls became the center of attention of their entire tribe during this happy time.

Afterward, the young women were regarded as eligible for marriage, and it was just a matter of time—a very short time in some tribes, up to several years in others—before they married. As one Sioux Indian said about the way his tribe lived early in the twentieth century, "Old timers got kids married right away. They tell them, 'You're ready for marrying now. You've got to get married.'" His father was about thirty, and his mother had just become a woman, when they got married.

Because Indians treated marriages basically as business contracts sealed with bride-wealth gifts and feasts, nobody invented songs and dances for weddings. But the rites of puberty and the courtship periods in the lives of young people had many festivities attached to them. Tribes staged not only feasts and elaborate, spiritually significant rituals for puberty, but other social events such as dances for adolescents. At dances, eligible young women met eligible young men.

Youngsters also devised other ways to meet, flirt, court and enjoy sex away from the prying eyes of their tribe's elders. Some tribes taught their young women that they had to remain virgins, or at least that they should be very careful to maintain an image of virginal behavior. Other tribes didn't ask their young women to uphold very strict standards, and the youngsters could enjoy love affairs rather openly, some of which culminated in marriage. Whether or not first love blossomed into marriages, the youngsters acquired experience that prepared them for mature relationships. When youngsters didn't have the benefit of early sexual experimentation before their marriages, they often had a very hard time adjusting to marriage partners. Sometimes they lived with their parents long after the wedding gifts were exchanged. In some tribes, couples even waited until they had children before they built their own lodgings and lived together. Parents had to help sheltered, frightened youngsters with no experience of intimacy to adjust to married life.

It was the rare tribe that encouraged extremely promiscuous behavior in their young people, or actually kept the boys and girls completely separate physically until their wedding days; however, those types of tribes did exist, too. The Blackfoot tolerated a great deal of sexual experimentation, while tribes in the

Pacific Northwest absolutely forbade it and kept the girls completely isolated during adolescence.

But when it came to the rites of puberty for girls, the tribes immediately immersed the girls in ceremonies that introduced them to their duties as women. In all the tribes, with the advent of puberty, the girls started to learn to do many chores that would become their responsibilities as wives and mothers.

Until they married, girls always lived with their mothers, or with their mother's or guardians' families. Boys lived with their mothers until adolescence, then they went to live with their fathers, or male relatives or guardians, to learn the skills required of grown men. A Pagago Indian woman in the early twentieth century remembered how her father, the chief of a village in southern Arizona, commanded the young men to run very long distances, as if in training for manhood. Men provided the raw materials of survival—animals and fish, animal skins and wood. But women faced the challenge of turning those materials into tipis and hogans, meals and clothes, moccasins, bags, baskets, blankets, shawls, and all kinds of implements and tools. Women were supposed to nurture their tribes during day-to-day life and support and inspire them through times of crisis. It's no wonder that part of the celebration of menarche virtually consecrated the young virgins to their lives as mature working women.

An excerpt from the autobiography of Maria Chono, who grew up in the old traditions of the Papago tribe in southern Arizona, conveys a taste of the superstitions and celebrations that a young woman faced when she reached puberty. (In the 1990s, the tribe renamed itself the Thohono O'odham.) She told chronicler Ruth Underhill:[1]

When I was nearly as tall as my mother, that thing happened to me which happens to all our women though I do not know if it does to the Whites. I never saw any signs. It is called menses.

Girls are very dangerous at that time. If they touch a man's bow, or even look at it, that bow will not shoot anymore. If they drink out of a man's bowl, it will make him sick. If they touch the man himself, he might fall down dead. My mother had told us this long ago, and we knew what had happened in our village.

There was a girl once who became dangerous and she did not tell. They were having a good time that day. All the village was planting in her father's field, and he had given them a meal of succotash. They were eating out in the field, her mother was cooking over a campfire. My mother was there and she said this girl was standing with a bowl in the crook of her arm, laughing and eating. It began to rain. The girl and her sisters ran home to take in the bedding, because we sleep out of doors in the summer and it was on the ground.

There was a crash of thunder. All the eating people stood still and then, from the house of that girl they heard a long sigh. They ran there. All the family were lying stunned on the floor, one sister was blind, and that girl was dead. The men dragged the people out into the rain and the house began to burn. 'See,' said those people, 'what has happened to us?' Her relatives buried that girl all alone and no one would go near.

Then there was a girl who was going to build a fire, and it seemed that it reached out, and took her, and burned her up. And there was another whose mother was struck by lightning. For it is not always you who are hurt if you commit this sacrilege; it may be anyone in your family.

That is why, when the lightning strikes a village, they send for the medicine man to see what woman was dangerous. He summons all the girls and looks at his crystals to see who did it. They do not punish that woman. It is enough to know that she has killed her friends.

Our mothers watch us, and so mine knew when it came to me. We always had the Little House ready, over behind our own house. It was made of some branches stuck in the ground and tied together at the top, with greasewood thrown over them to make it shady. There was no rain then, for it was winter, but it was cold in that Little House. The door was just big enough to crawl through, like our house door, and there was room for you to lie down inside, but not to stand up. My mother made me a new bowl and drinking cup out of clay, and put them in that house. When my mother cooked food at the big house, she would come over and pour some in my bowl, but no meat and nothing with salt in it. My father sharpened a little stick for me to scratch my hair with, because if I touched it, it would fall out. I was so afraid to lose my nice long hair that I kept that stick in my mouth all the time. Even when I was asleep, I had it there.

It was a hard time for us girls, such as the men have when they are being purified. Only they give us more to eat, because we are women. And they do not let us sit still and wait for dreams. That is because we are women, too. Women must work.

They chose my father's cousin to take care of me. She was the most industrious woman we had, always running with the carrying basket. That old woman would come for me in the dark when morning- stands-up. 'Come,' she said, 'Let's go for water over across the mountain. Let's go for firewood.'

So we would run far, far across the flat land and up the mountain and bring the water back before daylight; that old woman would talk to me.

'Work hard. If you do not work hard now, you will be lazy all your life. Then no one will want to marry you. You will have to take some good for nothing man for a husband. But if you are industrious, we shall find you a good old man.'

That is what we call our husbands: old man. But this woman did it out of modesty, too, so that I should not have young men in my mind. 'When you have an old man,' she said, 'you will grind the corn for him and you will always have water there for him to drink. Never let him go without water. Never let him go without food. He will go to the house of someone else to eat and you will be disgraced.'

I listened to her. Do you say that some girls might think of other things and not listen? But I wanted to be a good woman! And I have been. Ask anyone in our village if they ever saw me with idle hands. Or legs, either, when I was younger.

All the girls came around the Little House while that woman talked . . . (T)hey sat and listened and when she was tired of talking, they laughed and sang with me. And we played a game with little stones and a ball. We pick up the stones in different ways with one hand while we catch the ball in the other. Oh, we have good times at the Little House . . .

I had to stay four days and then I was not dangerous anymore. Everything goes by fours with our people, and Elder Brother arranged it that even this thing should be the same. No woman has trouble for more than four days. Then they gave me a bath just as they did to my father. Oh, it was cold in the winter time! I tell the girls who come of age in the summer they do not know what hardship is. The water even feels nice in summer.

My mother came in the dark of the morning with the water in a big new jar. The women had to run all day to get that water ready for me. I tried to get away but my mother caught me and made me kneel down. Then she dipped a gourd in the jar and poured that cold water down over my forehead.

"Hail!
I shall pour this over you.
You will be the one who endures cold.
You will think nothing of it."

It is true, I have never felt cold.

Then my mother washed my hair with soapweed fibres. That is the way women should always wash their hair and it will never grow gray. She cut it so it came just to my shoulders, for we women cannot have hair as long as the men; it would get in our way when we work. But we like to have it thick and shiny, and we know that everybody is noticing. There was quite a lapful that my mother cut off, and she saved it to make hair ropes for our carrying baskets. She had new clothes for me; two pieces of unbleached muslin, tied around my waist with a string. We did not know how to sew in those days . . .

Then I could go back to our house, only still I had to use the stick for four days and I could not eat salt. And then they danced me. All that month they danced me, until the moon got back to the place where it had been at first. It is a big time when a girl comes of age; a happy time. All the people in the village knew that I had been to the Little House for the first time, so they come to our house and the singer for the maidens came first of all.

That singer was the Chief's Leg, the man I told you about. He knew all the songs, the ones that Elder Brother first sang when he used to go over the country, dancing all the maidens. That Leg was the man who danced every maiden in our village when she came of age. His wife danced opposite him . . .

'Come out,' said my father on that first night. 'Now you must dance or the Leg will drag you out. He's mean.'

I did not want to dance; I was sleepy and I had run so far . . . But Luis, the Leg, came into the house and took me by the arm. He always danced next to the maiden, with his arm over her shoulders and the rattle in his other hand. He and I were at one end of a long line of people and his wife at the end of a line opposite. There was first a boy and then a girl, all down the line, with their arms over each other's shoulder and the blankets held along at the back. I told you the boys always like that dance."

The lines went to and fro, toward each other, and they kept wheeling a little, till at last they had made a circle . . .

. . . We had no fire; we kept warm dancing. After every four songs, Luis stopped, because his voice was hoarse. Then he let me go, and we girls went and sat together while the men smoked. How dark and cold it was then, with only one ember to light their cigarettes!

There were girls who did not come to sit with us and boys who did not sit with the men. How dark it was! Some mothers went looking for their girls in the night and some did not.

At midnight my mother brought jars of succotash. She had been cooking all day for this dance, and every day after that she cooked and ground corn and baked bread in the ashes. Every morning we gave gifts to Luis and his wife. My cut-off hair and dried beans and cooked food and the hand woven cotton that I wore for a dress. And to the girl friends who danced beside me, I gave my beads and my baskets because these people had suffered and endured sleeplessness with us.

We stopped dancing in the dark of the morning and then my mother said: 'Come and get firewood. Do you want to grow up as a lazy woman?' So then I went out in the dark to pick up the dead branches and bring them back before I slept. It seemed I slept only an hour before they were saying: 'Get up! Get water. Get wood. Grind the corn. If you sleep at this time you will be sleepy all your life.'

Oh, I got thin in that time! We girls are like strips of yucca fibre after our coming of age is over. Always running, and mostly gruel and ash bread to eat, with no salt. And dancing every night from the time the sun sets up until morning-stands-up. I used to go to sleep on Luis' arm and he pinched my nose to wake me . . ."

. . . At last the moon had come around again and they gave me a bath. It was over. I looked like half of myself. All my clothes were gone. All our dried corn and beans were eaten up. But I was grown up. Now the medicine man could cleanse me and give me a name.

You have to be cleansed as soon as the month is over; you must not wait. A cousin of mine did that once. She meant to be cleansed but she just waited. I think, perhaps, she did not have anything to pay the medicine man. But while she waited, one of her brothers was chopping wood. Something fell on him like a hot coal and killed him. So I went the day after my bath."

My mother and I went to the house of the medicine man early in the morning, with a big basket my mother had made, to pay him. He drew a circle on the ground and made me sit in it, cross-legged, with my back to the rising sun. In front of me he put a little dish. Then he walked away where we could not see him and took something out of a little deerskin bag. It was the clay that he carries to charm the evil away from women . . .

[To make the clay, the medicine man] grinds up the bone of a dead man and some owl feathers so that they are fine dust.

He put that clay in a tiny bowl in front before me, mixed with a little water. Then he walked up and down four times, facing the sun that was behind me. Every time he came up to me he blew over my head and dusted me off with . . . eagle feathers to brush away the evil. And every time he turned, he made a noise like an owl: hm. The fifth time, he took up the bowl of clay and stirred it around with a little owl feather that was standing in the center of it. Then he put the clay to my mouth. 'Drink this up!' So I drank it all.

Then he marked me, the sacred marks that are put on the men who have got salt from the magic ocean; the marks that take away bad luck and bring you a good life. On my breasts, on my shoulders, my back, and my belly.

'Your name shall be cha-veela.' I did not know before what name he was going to give me; neither did my parents. The medicine man names one from his dreams. Some of my friends had names that could be understood like Leaf Buds, Rustling Leaves, Windy Rainbow, Dawn Murmur. But I have never understood my name and he did not tell me.

After all that work, I did not menstruate again for a year!

⌒ ⌒

Maria Chono's tale addresses only the rites of *her* tribe, and yet they also contain elements of every tribe's celebration of puberty—the spiritual ceremonies, the isolation of the young women, the work ethic instilled in them from that time on, the dancing and the feasting and the physical exercises and hurdles a girl must face to become a woman. All the tribes, no matter how individualistic their approaches, include elements of the Papago rituals.

∽　∽

Among the Apaches, a girl's coming of age was cause for a jubilant celebration, too, with hair-cutting, singing, feasting and dancing. As late as July 1989, a puberty ceremony took place at the Mescalero Apache Reservation and the Fort Sill Apache Tribal Complex. The Apaches, being very hospitable, welcome visitors to this sort of celebration; although like most Indian tribes, the Apaches don't welcome observers into every aspect of their rites for this celebration and others. Some things are kept secret, for the Indians like to maintain their privacy. Even so, the author of *Women of the Apache Nation*, Henrietta Stockel,[2] tells of her experience at a puberty ceremony, to which she was invited.

On the reservation, passing by tall green pine trees and horses grazing, in a landscape dotted with tipis and tents, she traveled miles to an annual, group puberty ceremony. During the four days of the celebration, a rodeo was scheduled to take place.

"This rodeo is not like anything you've ever seen," said one old timer to a younger man in a conversation that the author overheard. "When the horn blows at the end of eight or ten seconds, the Apaches don't get off. They just hang on until they get thrown off or the animal quits, Apaches don't quit."[2]

The author noticed the rodeo bleachers on this hot day and, even more fascinating, a young Apache girl, perhaps only three years old, leading a tall, sturdy stallion across a field. What the child lacked in height—she came up only to the horse's knees—she made up for with the self-confident way she handled the horse.

The puberty ceremony began the next morning with the men of the tribe building a medicine tipi, a structure opening to the east. Unlike other tipis, this one had unpeeled lodgepolls. Neither the branches nor the bark was removed, and so the poles served as symbols as well as framework supports. "Closer to the ground, Apache men piled varieties of brush and up and down the lodgepoles, curling pliable smaller boughs around larger branches, creating vertical thickets that rose and descended along the entire height of the framework. Limbs, twigs, tendrils, all things green and leafy, went into the construction of the (tipi) that would enclose the maidens during the ceremony," wrote Stockel.[2]

The Apache women kept busy kneading dough and rounding it into tortillas, which they dropped into black cauldrons of bubbling, hot lard. The women used long forked sticks to manipulate the batter until it became brown, hard, traditional Apache fry bread.

Some tribes add powdered sugar, cinnamon, or honey to the fry bread, but the Apaches eat it in its natural state.

Throughout the four days of the ceremony, the families of the Apache girls coming of age provide food for everyone free of charge three times a day; the Indians serve boiled meat, beans, fry bread, mesquite pudding, and coffee or Kool-Aid. (Dancer Louis Mofsie, leader of the Thunderbird American Indian Dancers, a world famous troupe presenting authentic dances and songs of Native Americans, says the families of girls facing puberty rites always play host to guests in all tribes.)

At 8 A.M. on the first day, four young girls appeared; they wore buckskin dresses with exquisite bead designs, and beaded moccasins. A big entourage of people, godmothers, godfathers and sponsors, accompanied them. The girls crossed the ceremonial grounds, keeping their heads bowed and their hands folded in front of them. When they reached the medicine tipi, they kneeled on the greenery. Facing east, they received a blessing from the medicine men. Some portions of the rituals conducted inside the tent were kept secret from visitors' eyes, Stockel reported. But she knew that older women put pieces of buckskin on the ground. The girls lay face down on the skins. And the sponsors massaged the girls.

Set back up on their feet, the girls ran toward the east and "around a basket four times. After that,

Apache woven baskets full of candy and other trea-
sures, symbolizing abundance, were dumped over
the maidens' heads." Then trucks filled with candy
and fruit arrived. The girls' families had sent them.
The drivers threw the treats to the people. Then the
families of the maidens brought the feast food out
in large pots and served it. Afterward everyone,
including the maidens, took a break; they went to
their families' tipis.

Next came a parade with floats; a beautiful young
woman in an Apache beadwork tiara and traditional
Apache dress, rode in a long white limousine with flags
flying above her. She was Miss Mescalero of 1989. A
Navajo band dressed in white and turquoise satin costumes marched and played music. And a traditionally-
dressed Apache couple rode astride together on the
young man's horse.

In the afternoon, the rodeo began on time, but the
dancing contest was postponed and then canceled
because of the terrible heat. The Navajo Nation band
provided music. Dancing would take place at night,
when the day cooled off. At night, a fire was started,
and an announcer told people that they were about to
witness a festive but holy occasion.

With the sound of the tinkling of bells heralding
their approach, "four men with their chests and arms
painted black with white designs appeared. Wearing

fringed yellow buckskin skirts with jingles, and moccasins, they shuffled, single file, toward the fire. On their heads . . . were magnificent headdresses . . . In their hands they held short staffs painted with the symbols of a people long persecuted, yet vital, resilient, and rich in heritage." They pointed at the fire and danced around it. A clown followed them. And the dancers made a sound. "To the uninitiated it might have sounded like an owl's hoot," wrote the author, "but the notes were nearly soprano and were more of a call to or from the spirit world than an earthly harmonic. As they returned toward the fire in unending rhythm, a few women wrapped in shawls began to dance on the grounds . . ." The clown kept frolicking, entertaining the crowd. Then the maidens were taken to the medicine tent, where a fire hole had been dug in the ground and a fire begun. They went through more rites of puberty as the night progressed.

Indians throughout the country, including the Apaches, generally maintained very strict standards of behavior for menstruating women, who were supposedly at their most "powerful and dangerous" during that time. They were isolated in special housing, where the "negative force" of their blood would not overwhelm medicine, spoil crops or incapacitate warriors. Before re-entering society, they had to bathe. The same rules applied to women who had just delivered their babies. Women had no contact with men, crops or weapons during these times.[3]

⌒　⌒

Among the Navajos, and in most tribes, the rites of passage when a girl becomes a woman are the most important in her life. Girls wear traditional clothes and get their hair cut to a length just below their ears. Elders of the tribe groom a girl's hair with a special brush made of wheat. And every day at dawn, the girl must run toward the sun. Furthermore, on the first and last days of the celebration, an older woman in the tribe becomes a masseuse for the girl; the woman massages the girl's body with the aim of ridding it of its baby fat and childishness and imparting to it the strength of a woman's body.

On the last day of the celebration, family members, who have cooked an enormous corn cake sprinkled with cornmeal underground on hot rocks, serve it to guests. At the end of all the ceremonies, which include the feasting, the young woman becomes the newest link in the long chain of the tribe's ancestors back to its First Woman.[4]

⌒　⌒

Paul Radin, an expert on the Winnebago Tribe in Wisconsin, has written that it could be particularly cruel and even cannibalistic several centuries ago.[5] Nevertheless, the Winnebagos had many traditions, such as puberty customs, in common with less aggressive Native Americans.

Beginning when they were five, boys and girls listened to lectures about the customs of their ancestors. When the children reached adolescence, they were required to fast. For boys, fasting was the only rite of puberty. But it could be a tough one, because the boys had their faces blackened with charcoal and went to spend a night on a hill. Sometimes they went alone, sometimes with friends. Then they were sent back to spend two nights, then three nights on the hill. The boys were supposed to repeat the ritual until they were blessed; they were supposed to pray non-stop to the spirits to bless them.

When they faced this test, they could take either bread or charcoal with them. But if they chose the bread, their parents became angry, threw them out of the house, and tossed the charcoal out with them. Radin learned from an unnamed source that the boys usually took the bread and ran away into the wilderness; they did it to spite their parents, even though the boys ran the risk of being killed or captured by enemies. Parents wanted their sons to choose the charcoal so they would feel especially miserable and pray very intensely for a blessing.

One old man reminisced for Radin about how he and a friend were sent out as boys to fast on a hill together. They couldn't stop laughing at how funny they looked with their faces blackened with charcoal. On their way home, they used their saliva to streak their faces so they would look as if they had been crying and suffering.

Young girls fasted when they began to menstruate and had to spend time in menstrual lodges. Women went to the lodges from their first menstrual periods until the last time they menstruated. Winnebagos believed that menstruating women contaminated holy and sick people. So the women stayed apart, eating food cooked in separate fireplaces, using separate dishes from the rest of the tribe's. While a menstruating woman could have such dire effects on others and could even cause deaths, only one thing could hurt or kill her; that was known as a "war bundle," an entity that was wrapped in something from a cedar tree and used in "war bundle" feasts. The cedar may have contained poison, and that is why it was believed to be a cause of death for menstruating women.

Menstrual lodges stood close to the women's home lodges, so that their families could stay in touch with them. Sometimes the women's lovers visited the menstrual lodges and had sexual trysts. Unwelcome men might try to visit the women, too, and their families tried to protect them. Radin's informant said that families especially wanted to guard their women against "ugly" men, who usually had love potions, which were very difficult, perhaps impossible, to fight against.

There seemed to be no end to the superstitions that Winnebago women had to deal with when they menstruated. They had to take their blankets with them to the lodges, wrap themselves in the blankets, and sit up for their entire stays. They weren't permitted to look out at the daylight or the sky, for fear that the weather would turn very bad. They weren't allowed to eat or drink anything for four days. They weren't allowed to touch their own bodies, except with a stick, or else they would become sick. (Other tribes, too, had scratching sticks for menstruating women.) When a woman's menstrual flow stopped, she bathed herself and put on new clothes. Her family purified their home with red cedar leaves and performed other sanctifying rites. Then the woman could go back to her family's lodge.

As soon as a young girl went through her first menstrual period, she was considered ready to be courted and married. Radin, hearing about menstrual period customs, thought it was very odd that women could meet their lovers in the menstrual lodges. But Winnebago women were protected only against the visits by unworthy men, Radin was told. The women may have been married to their visiting lovers, or may have simply been considered married after the visits, or else the couple married shortly after the woman left the menstrual lodge. Girls were definitely married soon after they reached puberty.

Usually parents arranged the marriages, and the children rarely protested. But if a child didn't want to marry a particular person, the parents didn't force the match. As with many other tribes, the Winnebagos had no wedding ceremony except for an exchange of gifts.

NOTES

1. *Native American Autobiography: An Anthology*, The University of Wisconsin Press, Madison, Wisconsin, 1994. This excerpt comes from Chapter 18, "Autobiography of a Papago Woman," edited by Ruth Underhill, in Part 5: "The Anthropologists' Indians, 1900 . . ."

   The anthology notes that Maria Chono was the daughter of a Tucson chief in a village called Mesquite Root west of Tucson. She learned to weave baskets, as all the women in her tribe did. She also had an uncommonly independent spirit. The tribe, which was divided between Arizona and Mexico, was primarily Catholic from its contacts with the Spanish, but it also retained its beliefs in the teachings of its own, older faith. Ruth Underhill interviewed Maria Chono in the early 1930s. Underhill spoke a few words of Papago, and Chono knew some Spanish. Chono's account of her life depends heavily on the translation and interpretation of white people; her tale is essentially a composite.

2. *Women of the Apache Nation*, by H. Henrietta Stockel, University of Nevada Press, Reno, Nevada, 1991.

3. *Weaving New Worlds: Southeastern Cherokee Women and Their Basketry*, by Sarah H. Hill, The University of North Carolina Press, Chapel Hill, N.C., and London.
4. *Navajo*, by Susanne and Jake Page, Harry N. Abrams, Publishers, New York, 1995.
5. *The Winnebago Tribe*, by Paul Radin, University of Nebraska Press, Lincoln, Nebraska, and London, England, 1990, originally published as part of the Thirty-Seventh Annual Report of the Bureau of American Ethnology, Smithsonian Institution, Washington, 1923.

9

DANCES AND POWWOWS

Louis Mofsie, a Hopi-Winnebago Indian by heritage, leader and founder of the Thunderbird American Indian Dancers, travels all over the United States, Israel and Japan, dancing with his troupe gathered from many tribes. He wants to preserve the traditions and educate other people about the great artistic legacy and culture of Native Americans. Schedules of his group's spectacular, exciting performances done in authentic costumes are usually available from the American Indian Community House and the National Museum of the American Indian. Sometimes Mofsie's group dances at the Theater for the New City in New

York City, among other performance spaces in the New York City and other locations in the Northeast.

Native Americans celebrate their weddings with feasts, just as everyone else does. There aren't any special dances for weddings. However, Native Americans do have some special dances for the rites of puberty. One such dance is the "Mountain Spirit Dance," danced by the spirits of the four sacred mountains of the Apaches in Arizona, in a desert area surrounded by mountains. Information about the dance is available, listed under the "Mountain Spirit Dance of the Apaches," in books in stores, at the National Museum for the American Indian and at libraries, such as several university libraries with literature on Native Americans.

Mofsie used to perform the Mountain Spirit Dance with his Thunderbird dancers, but he no longer does, because he has been advised by the Apaches that they want to keep it private. Not every tribe has dances or songs for its rites of puberty, but every tribe considers the rites themselves as a blessing.

However, there's one dance, called the round dance, squaw dance, or circle dance (they're all the same) that everyone is welcome to witness and take part in these days. It usually closes the powwows, which take place all over the country, sponsored by many tribes and open to the public. The circle dance was originally used to introduce young men and women when they reached adolescence. Young women held hands, and so did the young men, dancing a simple, shuffle step, in rings around each other. Ordinarily men and women didn't dance or sing together. Drums and rattles have provided most of the accompaniment for the harsh-toned, non-harmonic Native American singing and for the dancing, too—both usually performed only by the men. Young men did play flutes as a melody instrument, but the flutes were used primarily for courting. Native Americans usually used music for rituals and ceremonies connected with religion, farming, hunting, fishing, warring, medical, puberty, and funeral rites, and other life cycle rituals. Women sang lullabies. And they had their own less dramatic, simple style of dancing in their own social groups. To a much lesser extent, Native Americans occasionally used singing and dancing, either as individuals, or in groups, strictly for pleasure.

As an historic sidelight, Indian drumming definitely influenced jazz. To what degree is unknown. But many Native Americans and African Americans intermarried, and in some ways their cultures blended. American Indian drumming techniques are believed to have had a great impact on African American rhythmic techniques and innovations for jazz.

In any case, powwows are among the best places to see Indian dances these days, hear the drums, watch the Native Americans compete and struggle to maintain their traditions, reach out to communicate with and play host to non-Indians. At powwows, Native Americans usually sell a variety of crafts. Most Americans don't know about powwows. But for the original inhabitants of the United States, powwows are part ritual, part homecoming—a combination of fiesta, Fourth of July, and Thanksgiving, and a reaffirmation of Native American identity. At powwows, Native Americans of all tribes gather to celebrate their cultures, confirm their identities, dance, feast, and greet old friends and make new ones.

According to the U.S. Census, there are only about a million and a half Indians, including Americans, Eskimos, and Aleuts—a relatively small number but double the estimated number in 1890. About half these people live on reservations: 45 million acres of territory set aside for their use in Alaska, and 50 million in the lower 48 American states. So it's not always easy to know where the celebrations are. If you know where to look, however, you'll find yourself thrilling to the powerful sound of the powwow drums far in the distance. The drumbeat pulls at everyone's pulse. You'll hear the chanting, too, and then see dancers in breathtaking costumes—furred, feathered, flashing with beadwork and enhanced by face paint. You'll have the chance to join in what might be called the oldest kind of party in America.

Powwows are held all over the U.S., and they take place year-round. Drums call New Englanders to the Fourth of July powwow held by the Wampanoag Indians in Mashpee, Massachusetts on Cape Cod, to the lavish celebration at United Tribes Technical College in Bismarck, North Dakota, during late summer, to the large and splendid Oklahoma, New Mexico, and Montana powwows, and to the Labor Day powwow of the Shinnecocks on their reservation in Southampton, on Long Island, in New York, which has become a nearly obligatory media event, since it's larger than most powwows in the most media-saturated area in the U.S. Altogether there are a couple of hundred powwows a year in the U.S.

Tribes differ a great deal in clothes, food, dances and chants. Some Indian languages can be as incomprehensible from tribe to tribe as Turkish is to the French. And tribes have different powwow traditions. For example, the Wampanoags of Massachusetts never used a drum until the twentieth century. They were fishermen and hunters, who were given a piece of land in Mashpee, one of the first reservations, as a reward for staying neutral in some kind of war Europeans waged against each other in seventeenth century North America. The drums came from the Plains tribes, among them the war-making tribes, the Sioux, Pawnees and Omahas.

In the 1930s, federal laws barring Native Americans from preserving their cultures were lifted. What's more, improved transportation made it easier for everyone, including Indians, to travel. Tribes visited each other's festivals. By now their dances, songs, customs, skills and talents have formed a brimming pool of pan-Indian culture.

Indian tribes have centuries-old religious ceremonies, to which non-Indians are not invited. These include dances celebrating harvests and rainfalls, as well as, of course, the life passages for boys and girls arriving at adulthood and preparing for marriage. Non-Indians can see some of these dances in the repertory of the Thunderbirds. And some traditional dances have undergone metamorphoses. Indians at their powwows have evolved pan-Indian dances, in the tribes' attempts to preserve their cultures by presenting a united social front.

The Gourd or Grass dance, originally a war dance done only by Plainsmen dressed in elaborate costumes including eagle feathers for headdresses and waist bustles, and blades of grass intertwined in the regalia, changed into an animated Fancy Dance. A circle, which women used to form around the dancing warriors, became the Round Dance, or Squaw Dance, or Circle Dance—a welcoming dance with everyone invited to join. The dance, a simple, side-moving step, starts and finishes many powwows now and also provides entertainment after the scheduled events end at the powwow grounds late each night.

Many Indians, who normally stay in motels as everybody else does, bring their own tipis, traditional, decorated tents first developed by the Plains Indians, and pitch them at outdoor powwows. That way, they can stay up late for the Round Dances, which signify the oneness of all people. "The 49ers (Round Dances) are so popular, they often attract more people than the official powwows," Louis Mofsie has said with a smile, remembering his observations of dances and powwows across the country.

For non-Indians, powwows are educational entertainment as varied as the regions in which the tribes live. The powwows also afford opportunities for non-Indians to observe traditions they can bring home to adapt for their own ceremonies and parties. They can watch such things as the Gourd Dance to honor veterans. Indians have sent an impressive number of servicemen, most of them volunteers, to the country's wars—12,000 in World War I, before Indians had citizenship. More than double that number went to World War II, where some of them used the Navajo language as an unbreakable code to stymie the Japanese. "Indians were awarded 71 Air Medals, 51 Silver Stars, 47 Bronze Stars, 34 Distinguished Flying Crosses, and two Congressional Medals of Honor," wrote Arlene Hirschfelder in her prize-winning book, *Happily May I Walk.*[1]

The Gourd Dance may be adopted or performed at non-Indian celebrations, such as weddings. And visitors to powwows can watch the "give-aways," presents of blankets and beadwork, which Indians simply give to each other in a show of generosity. Similar give-aways can be featured by non-Indians in their own celebrations, especially weddings. Indian crafts or bead work items would make lovely gifts for wedding guests.

To the dismay of some Indians, powwows are becoming commercialized. Powwow directors try to monitor booths to ensure they are manned by Native Americans and sell only genuine Native American arts and crafts. Dancers sometimes cause controversy. Professionals sometimes appear to compete in contests for the best dancing and finest costumes. Prizes can range from $2000 to well over $5000.

Many Indians long for the days when people danced for joy instead of profit. Competitions to prove superiority contradict Indian ideas, they say. But powwow organizers know that attendance would fall off without the contests. One Sioux, who has competed as a dancer at Plains powwows, summed up his spirit, which blends modern goals with respect for the old ways. "I read of old warriors and their eagle feathers. They got themselves psyched up before they went into battle. I read where they danced in animal costumes to get the adrenaline flowing. They danced in a circle and never backed up, because a warrior never backs up." The modern contestants dance with fervor. And the booty from this "war" is an income for people who work to perpetuate Native American culture.

Helpful Hints for Incorporating Traditional Dances and Powwow Customs into the Wedding Celebration:

SOME couples may choose to hire traditional dancers to perform at their wedding reception. Perhaps the bride and groom could do a little research and perform a traditional dance as their "first dance." Others in the wedding party, the bridesmaids and groomsmen, for example, may want to perform their own dances as well.

Another idea is to hire musicians or a band that specializes in Native American music and songs. Many guests may enjoy their first taste of Native American musical tradition at a wedding. See the resource information on powwows below.

POWWOWS:

Here are a few notable powwows where people can go to observe and bring back ideas, crafts, and customs to add to their own engagement and wedding parties. In some cases, powwows charge an entrance fee.

Alaska: The World Eskimo Indian Olympics, Fairbanks, Alaska, are always held during a weekend in July. Native Americans from the north compete in Arctic skills, sports and dance contests. A favorite "soul food" here is whale blubber, which gives new meaning to the phrase "chew the fat." The phone number is 907-452-6646.

Massachusetts: The Mashpee Wampanoag Powwow, Mashpee, Mass., is held over the Fourth of July weekend. It attracts Native Americans from all over the country. Visitors should definitely make a point of sampling the plum porridge served there. The powwow ends with a worship service and a clambake. Write Powwow, c/o Tribal Council, Mashpee, Mass. 02649. The phone number is 508-477-0208.

New York Area: Long Island hosts the Shinnecock Powwow in Southampton, New York, over the Labor Day weekend. For exact dates, call the American Indian Community House, 212-598-0100.

Montana: The Crow Fair, on the Crow reservation about 65 miles from Billings, attracts a big crowd to a parade, rodeo, dances, and a feast. For information, write or call the Crow Agency. The address is Crow Tribal Council, Crow Agency, P.O. Box 159, Montana 59022. Attention: Alberta Rides The Horse. The phone number is 406-638-2601.

⌒　⌒

New Mexico: The Gathering of Nations Powwow takes place in April, with dozens of events and thousands of participants. Call or write the Gathering of Nations Information Office, c/o Box 75102, Station 14, Albuquerque, N.M. 87194. The phone number is 505-836-2810. Or you can also call the Albuquerque Conference and Visitors Bureau, phone 505-842-9918.

The Gallup Ceremonial in Red Rock State Park is an outdoor event renowned for Southwestern crafts as well as for dancing and a rodeo. The event focuses primarily on the northern and southern Plains Indians, whose horsemanship is something close to perfection, and features some of the finest riding and roping in the West. Write the Intertribal Indian Ceremonial Association, 226 W. Cole Ave., Gallup, N.M. 87301. The phone number is 505-863-3896.

Other sources of information in New Mexico are: The Indian Pueblo Cultural Center, phone number

1-800-766-4405, and the Visitors Bureau, phone number 1-800-284-2282, both in Albuquerque.

⌒⌒   ⌒⌒

North Dakota: The United Tribes Powwow, Bismarck, takes place on the weekend after Labor Day. This is a traditional Plains Indian celebration and ceremonial, complete with tipis and Buffalo meat. The war bonnet originated in these parts and can be seen here in all its glory. Contact the United Tribes Technical College, 3315 University Drive, Bismarck, N.D. 58504. The phone number is 701-255-3285 between 1 and 5 P.M. on weekdays.

⌒⌒   ⌒⌒

Oklahoma: Many powwows take place in this state on the weekends. The American Indian Exposition, in Anadarko, takes place in August, featuring greyhound and horse races and a parade. For information, contact the Chamber of Commerce, Debbie Riddle, 405-247-6651.

For other powwows in the state, call the different tribes—the Comanches in Elgin, Oklahoma, phone number 580-492-3786; the Apaches in Apache, Oklahoma, phone number 580-588-2298; the Kiowas in Carnegie, Oklahoma, phone number 580-654-2328; and the Wichita Tribe in Anadarko, 405-247-2425. And there are others. Powwows are held for a variety of reasons; some held by churches, or schools, or individual families to honor a person; some are fundraisers. The Red Earth powwow/arts and crafts festival is usually held in June in Oklahoma City in the Myriad Convention Center, One Myriad Gardens, Oklahoma City 73102, phone 405-297-3000. Also for information, call the Chamber of Commerce, phone number 405-297-8900, and the Red Earth Festival, phone 405-427-5228.

For a complete guide to powwows, consult the Powwow Directory available as either a bimonthly newsletter or a biannual volume, from Indian Country Communications, c/o Lac Courte Oreilles Reservation, 7831N Grindstone Ave., Hayward, Wisconsin 54843. The phone is 715-634-5226, open Monday through Friday year round. A subscription costs $35/year for the newsletter on a continuing basis, or the biannual volume costs $2. for one issue. The newsletter has the advantage of including updates for powwows, which sometimes change their dates.

NOTE

1. *Happily May I Walk*, Arlene Hirschfelder, Charles Scribner's Sons, New York, 1987.

❧ **10** ❧
FOOD

For planning meals for all kinds of parties associated with engagements and weddings, recipes derived from homey, earthy, traditional Native American foods can provide a lively alternative to familiar cuisine styles. The Indians were ingenious about discovering nutritious and often tasty foods provided by nature in the wilderness, in virtually every climate. Thousands of years before Christ, Indians began preparing wild corn and devising countless ways to cook and serve it as food, food additives and enhancers, soups, and drinks.

Botanists digging in a cave in New Mexico in the twentieth century found ears of maize that they analyzed and believed were about 5000 years old. Then they found a newer form of cultivated, cross-bred corn, which they believed originated around the year 1 A.D. Long before white settlers came to North America, most Native Americans regarded corn as a staple of their diet.

They boiled, toasted, baked, fried, and roasted it. They mixed it with meat, fish, and vegetables that they both grew and found in the wild, plus fruits and nuts. They ground corn into flour for bread and cake, thickened soups with it, included it in their stews, and invented corn porridge and succotash among other corn-based foods. The white settlers adopted some of them, most notably succotash and corn bread. The saga of corn in the lives of the Native Americans probably began when traders brought wild corn from Central to North America.

In the Pacific northwest, Native Americans didn't rely upon corn, beans, or squash, as many tribes in the rest of the country did. In the northwest, Native Americans dined on wild plants, roots, berries and nuts, acorns in particular, accompanying their primary diet of fish, especially salmon, which they prepared in many ways and stored in great quantities, and shellfish and small game. Although they weren't great fans of plants and vegetables, they did like a plant related to the hyacinth. With a nutritious, edible bulb, it became a staple of their diet. Seafood was important on the Gulf of Mexico and the East Coast, too—much more important than vegetables and plants.

Indians learned from observation of the effects of foods that meat was very important in their diet, and a source of protein, by whatever name they called it. So they ate few meals that didn't include some kind of meat. They also knew about the value of a balanced diet. Many agricultural tribes served corn and beans, both of them secondary sources of protein, along with meat. And they also knew they had to include starch, sugar, and fats in their meals and learned which plants, both those found in the wild and others which they cultivated, contained the nutrients they needed.

Tribes regarded berries as important in the Northwest and had many ways of preparing them. Sometimes they cooked berries into a pulpy mass and dried them into cakes. Some tribes even devised watertight baskets for boiling. The Southwestern tribes were masterful basket makers. And many tribes discovered they could place food on top of hot stones buried in large, shallow pits, cover them with leaves and mats, and steam the food by pouring water through to the stones.

Acorns were a staple food for the majority of the primitive California tribes. They devised many ways of cooking and storing acorns; though some of their concoctions were tasteless, they provided nutrients.

Of all the wild animals the Indians hunted, they valued the buffalo the most, for they could use every part of it, except for its snout, for baking, boiling, and roasting. One Spanish explorer, writing about his first taste of buffalo (or bison) in the sixteenth century, thought it was a finer and fatter animal than cattle in his own country. Buffalo ranged from the Rockies in the west to the Allegheny Mountains in the east, and from Canada in the north to Mexico in the south.

"Tongues, eyes, brains, tripe, hearts, and other internal organs were eaten," write John Lipton Terrell and Donna M. Terrell in their book *Indian Women of the Western Morning*,[1] "Blood and fat went into puddings, stews, soups, and other dishes. Fetal calves, when very small, were considered a great delicacy. Bone marrow, extracted by cracking large, roasted bones, was savored by all Indians. Some relished lungs boiled with corn. Others were especially fond of grilled udder, with or without the milk in it."

One Indian woman shared her recipe for buffalo blood broth with an anthropologist. The recipe included blood, water, marrow fat, and dried cooked squash, to be stirred by a stick made from a chokecherry sapling for extra flavoring. The cooking time lasted until all traces of the blood disappeared.

After the buffalo, of all the game available, deer, antelope, and elk were the animals of choice.

On the prairies of the Midwest and the Great Plains, Native Americans loved onions and turnips, which mixed easily with other foods and made them tasty. And the Indians found them easy to store. Among other popular foods were strawberries, gooseberries, artichokes, cherries, and plums. Usually the tribe's older women and youngest girls did the berry, fruit and vegetable picking. When they discovered an especially abundant cache of vegetables, whole families, including the men, joined in the harvesting.

Native Americans loved game birds, too. In season, particularly in the spring and fall, ducks and geese migrated over the United States, and so did other birds. Some tribes maintained flocks of domesticated turkeys, and there were also wild turkeys in the south and southeast.

In the east, where tribes had a varied menu of fish, game, corn, wild fruits and plants, they used mushrooms as a basis for bread baking. That was true all along the coast from New England to the deep South. And New Englanders tapped maple trees for the sap to make sugar and syrup.

In the southwest, the Hopi tribe discovered that mixing salty clay with some bitter foods made them edible. The Hopi also used cactus fruits and dried squash to enliven the taste of food and make up for a lack of sugar sources in their arid area.

From the corn soups of the southern tribes to the tasty creations of the Plains tribes, simple and elegant soups as a first course could be a great way to introduce your guests to a Native American appetizer. It could very well be the most exotic soup ever served at an engagement or wedding party. Here are some recipe ideas:

NATIVE AMERICAN HOMINY SOUP
(from the Southern Tribes)

¼ pound salt pork or bacon
1 onion, peeled and sliced
2 (1 pound 13-ounce) cans hominy
1 quart buttermilk
½ teaspoon (or to taste) salt
freshly ground black pepper, to taste
fresh chopped parsley or chives, for garnish

- ♨ Sauté salt pork or bacon in a large stock pot over medium heat until cooked. Drain the fat.
- ♨ Add onion to the pot, and sauté until golden.
- ♨ Stir in hominy and continue to cook over medium-low heat, stirring occasionally, for 5 minutes.
- ♨ Add buttermilk, and salt and pepper. Continue to cook over medium-low heat for an additional 5 minutes. Be sure not to bring the soup to a simmer. Remove salt pork or bacon before serving. Serve the

soup warm, not hot, garnished with chopped chives or parsley.

MAKES 8 TO 10 SERVINGS.

Another variation of corn soup comes from the Plains Indians:

DRIED CORN SOUP

1 ear dried blue and white or yellow corn (remove
    kernels from the cob)
1 slice bacon
2¹/₂ ounces dried beef, chopped finely
freshly ground black pepper to taste

- Soak corn in 2 cups water for 48 hours.
- Place corn, along with its soaking water, in a large stock pot or saucepan. Add 5 cups water and bacon slice. Simmer, covered, for 3¹/₂ to 4 hours, or until the corn is tender but not soft.
- Add dried beef and pepper and cook for 10 minutes more.
- Serve hot.

MAKES 6 SERVINGS.

This elegant consommé is an alternative to a corn-based soup:

CONSOMMÉ OF TROUT

8 cooked trout heads
1 teaspoon salt
freshly ground black pepper, to taste
2 tablespoons chopped fresh parsley, for garnish

♨ Combine trout heads, 5 cups water, salt and pepper in a stock pot. Simmer for 30 minutes.
♨ Strain soup and garnish with parsley before serving. (This soup may also be served cold as an aspic).

MAKES 4 TO 6 SERVINGS.

The Apache obtained nourishing foods from wild plants, among them some cactus fruits, piñon nuts, bulbs and roots of many kinds, mesquite beans, mushrooms, greens, berries, acorns and seeds.

Indians thought very highly of their diet and considered it superior to foods eaten by white people. As Maria Chono recalled, she began grinding seeds as a very young girl, and her mother made gruel out of wild seeds: "wild seeds and cactus, those are the good foods," she said.

Several cookbooks focus on Native American cooking. Presented in a very sophisticated, comprehensible way, *New Native American Cooking* by Dale Carson[2] has easy-to-follow directions for appetizers, soups, chowders and stews, bread, fish and shellfish, fowl and game, vegetables, starches and side dishes, condiments and preserves, desserts, and beverages. Ms. Carson bases all her recipes on traditional Native American foods such as corn, tomatoes, beans, squash, berries, maple syrup, varieties of game, meats and fowl, fish and shellfish, plus other foods that Native Americans worked into their own repertoire, such as apples, wheat and oat flour, leavening, dairy products, and eggs.

The author doesn't consider her book to be an authentic history of Native American food, because she does include elements that purists with expertise about Indian foods would omit. Instead she regards her book as a bridge to introduce Native American food traditions into the mainstream.

And so she has given clear directions for preparing such dishes as oysters on the half shell, stuffed quahogs, mussels with lemon-butter (definitely not a Native American dish—this is bridge food), smoked halibut cheeks, and wild mushroom appetizer, to name only a few items. First of all, she warns people not to go picking wild mushrooms. She herself loves to cook big, chewy portobello mushrooms to serve with buffalo, beef, veal, or oysters.

Below is a mushroom and salmon recipe that would serve as a very tasty appetizer at a wedding reception. This dish hints at authentic Native American food, while suggesting an elegance that could enhance anyone's dinner party.

MUSHROOMS STUFFED WITH
MISHQUAMMAUQUOCK
(Salmon)

20 large fresh button mushrooms
1 tablespoon hazelnut oil
$1/4$ cup finely chopped green onion or scallions
2 tablespoons finely chopped hazelnuts, walnuts
   or pecans
$1/2$ teaspoon fresh dillweed
$1/2$ teaspoon Worcestershire sauce
$1/4$ teaspoon salt
dash hot pepper sauce
4 ounces smoked or steamed salmon, flaked OR the
   contents of 1 ($6^1/2$-ounce) can boneless, skinless
   pink salmon, drained, picked clean, and flaked
   salmon roe and minced fresh flat-leaf parsley
   for garnish

🔥 Clean mushrooms and remove stems and dark spots.

🔥 Place half the mushrooms, stem side up, around the edge of a glass pie plate. Cover with waxed paper and microwave for 3 to 4 minutes, or until the mushrooms are almost tender and starting to render liquid. Or, place half the mushrooms on a pie plate, cover with aluminum foil, and bake at 350°F for 10 minutes. Invert cooked mushrooms on paper towels to drain. Repeat with remaining mushrooms.

🔥 In a bowl, stir together hazelnut oil, onion, nuts, dill, Worcestershire sauce, salt, and hot pepper sauce. Stir in the salmon.

🔥 Fill the mushroom caps with the salmon mixture, rounding the tops.

🔥 Place the filled mushrooms around the edge of the glass plate and microwave, uncovered, about 2½ minutes, giving the plate a half turn about halfway through the cooking time. Or, return the filled mushrooms to a 350°F oven and bake for 3 to 5 minutes, or until the salmon mixture is bubbly.

🔥 Garnish with salmon roe and parsley. Serve immediately.

MAKES 6 TO 8 SERVINGS.

⌐— —⌐

Here is a recipe for a distinctive salad dressing that could also enhance a first course of fresh greens.

MAPLE-MUSTARD VINAIGRETTE

$1/4$ cup vegetable oil
$1/2$ cup walnut oil
$3/8$ cup cider vinegar
$1^{1}/_{2}$ tablespoons maple syrup
1 tablespoon coarse brown mustard
salt and freshly ground black pepper, to taste

⚜ In a small mixing bowl, combine all the ingredients and whisk together until smooth and emulsified.
⚜ Pour into a serving dish or store, covered, in the refrigerator for up to 5 days.

⌒   ⌒

Dale Carson also invented a Native American antipasto, including raw clams and oysters, smoked trout, grilled roasted herring, lobster and crab in cider-hazelnut vinaigrette, sliced buffalo sausage, and a few other items, like pemmican and squawbread, for which there are recipes in her book. You can use as few or as many of the above ingredients as you prefer. The antipasto can pass muster simply with marinated Jerusalem artichokes, tomatoes, roasted bell peppers, sautéed wild mushrooms, batter dipped greens, roasted corn on the cob (with the cobs cut in quarters,) and walnut or hazelnut oil, chopped nuts, and minced herbs. (The book has recipes for all these ingredients.) Assemble all the items on a large platter and drizzle with nut oil and sprinkle with chopped nuts and minced herbs, and serve. It will certainly make an impressive first course and add a special flair to your engagement or wedding celebration.

Among the soups included are Black Bean Soup with Native Herbs, Wild Rice Soup, a Winter Root and Onion Soup, Fish Chowder, Oyster Stew, Mushroom Soup, Sorrel Soup a la Sioux, Sweet Potato Soup with Corn and Chilis, Butternut Squash Soup, Watercress and Potato Soup, Buffalo Ragout which can also be done with rump or eye of round beef, and Buffalo Sausage Stew with Roasted Barley and Onions.

There are Crawfish and Black Bean Cakes among the fish recipes; and among the game dishes, Roast Wild Duck with Blackberry Sauce, Smoked Wild Turkey, and recipes for venison and buffalo sausages— and many more.

There's a good recipe for succotash (corn and beans together). In the days of the Plymouth colony in Massachusetts, succotash was a soup containing fowl as well as corn and beans. Cooks can perform many variations on the theme of succotash. The author, of Abenaki Indian heritage, has a Cherokee friend who makes succotash with green beans, fresh tomatoes, onions, and corn kernels tossed with fresh herbs. The author grew up in the east, eating succotash with corn kernels, lima beans, butter, and cream.

Powwows have spread the word about Apache frybread. It can be served in its natural state. Ms. Carson suggests topping it with honey or jam. Frybread can be cooked with yeast, or baking soda, or oil, or butter. The author's recipe is:

FRYBREAD

1 tablespoon vegetable oil, for frying
2½ cups flour
½ teaspoon salt
1 teaspoon baking powder
½ teaspoon sugar
1 teaspoon oil
1 cup warm milk

- Heat oil in skillet until hot, but not smoking, over medium-high heat.
- In a large bowl, combine the rest of the ingredients to make a dough. Shape into disks.
- Fry shaped dough in hot oil until browned and crispy.
- Serve hot.

MAKES 8 TO 10 FIVE-INCH DISCS.

The frybread can definitely provide a surprising

alternative to plain dinner rolls or Italian bread at any dinner party.

Helpful Hints for Adding a Taste of Authentic Native American Cuisine to a Wedding Dinner:

RECIPES for canapés and all sorts of appetizers, main courses, side dishes, especially those made with corn, will add the natural and simple goodness of Indian cooking to your celebration. Visit your local bookstore or library to search for Native American cookbooks to get some more ideas for recipes.

It may be helpful to include menu cards on each table, describing the different dishes that will be served and their significance. You could also decorate these menu cards with Native American drawings or patterns.

Instead of the traditional floral centerpiece on each table, why not create your own Native American-inspired centerpiece? You could include pumpkins, squashes, gourds, dried corn (perhaps different colors), dried peppers, feathers, shells, beads and leaves in handmade baskets. You may even want to spread each table with a traditional cloth or hand-woven tapestry, and include traditional pottery, instruments, or other handicrafts as the centerpiece.

As a party favor, you could make a little "book" for each guest, including the recipes for the dishes that are served at the wedding reception. If you know the name of the recipe in the original language, you could add it in for a special touch. You could even include some traditional love poetry or love songs. Reproducing Native American artwork on the cover of the booklet, and tying it together with rattan will give your guests a unique "artifact" and souvenir of your celebration.

NOTES

1. *Indian Women of the Western Morning*, by James Lipton Terrell and Donna M. Terrell, Anchor Books, New York, 1976, originally published by The Dial Press, New York, 1974.
2. *New Native American Cooking*, by Dale Carson, Random House, New York, 1996.

11

FASHIONS, JEWELRY, BASKETRY, CLOTH WEAVING AND DECORATIONS

"**W**hat do Native American women wear for their weddings?" a writer recently asked Georgetta Ryan, a reference librarian at the National Museum of the American Indian in New York.

"They wear their best stuff," she replied. She chose a magnificent silver and turquoise belt depicted in a book on the subject of fine Indian jewelry. "Men would wear that, too," she said. But Native Americans have a vast number of praiseworthy choices. Everything depends on individual taste.

Native Americans have earned well-deserved international fame for their basket-making, weaving of cotton cloth and wool for clothes, blankets, and other decorative and utilitarian uses, preparation of animal skins for clothes and tents, and for their artistry as designers and jewelry makers. In the Southwest, the men were the cloth weavers, and they created designs—illustrations, really—of representative figures of people and animals. Women made the baskets, and their designs were always abstract and geometrical.

All Native American tribes created and wore jewelry. It could be made from beads, feathers, shells, fresh water pearls, carved wood and other materials, and, most distinctive of all, jewelry made from silver, turquoise and coral. In the Southwest, the Zuni wrought magnificent jewelry of museum quality. Their rings, necklaces, bracelets, belts, and other pieces can sell for very high prices. The Navajo may have become silversmiths before the Zuni in the 19th century, but the Zuni people developed their craft of jewelry making to such a high art that they influenced the techniques and imaginations of the Navajo. They became topnotch jewelry makers, too.

The artistry of Native American jewelry makers has become a subject of serious study on the university level. The same is true of their basketry making, weaving, and visual designing. In the modern world, with commercialism in mind, Native Americans have even put their imprint on such items as bow ties and cummerbunds for bright, distinctive formal evening wear. Often Indian arts and crafts are sold at pow-wows, as well as in stores and museum shops. A shop at the National Museum of the American Indian has a wide variety of items for home decoration and fashion wear, including the cummerbunds and bow ties.

The arts and crafts of Native Americans can constitute a lifelong study. Readers can acquaint themselves with the crafts and jewelry available for sale by referring to the books listed at the end of this chapter.

In the southwest, Native American women first wove baskets and worked in ceramics, making all kinds of pots, jars, platters and utensils. They actually began to develop their skills thousands of years ago, and so did Native American women living far to the east. They probably first learned their craft when traders brought examples of objects from South to North America a long time ago.

By the time the first white settlers arrived in Indian lands, basketry, created by coiling, braiding, and twining, had become a highly developed art. Women also made mats, bags, and boxes; they didn't wear clothes with pockets, and they needed bags to carry all kinds of tools. Women learned how to weave baskets so tightly that they could hold water; when the women put hot rocks inside, these watertight baskets could cook food. Women were very inventive in making designs for their baskets, some of which even included beads and shells. And the women used all sorts of natural sources for coloring their designs.

Native Americans all around the country also learned weaving and spinning with handlooms, probably from Europeans, and particularly from Spaniards in the southwest. Women often did the weaving work, too, except among the Hopis, where the Hopi men were the great weavers. All of them produced wool clothes and blankets, employing all kinds of materials such as bird feathers and animal skins to beautify their designs. Some weavers even used buffalo hair. In the southwest, the Hopis wove cotton cloth, while other tribes wove other materials. Hopi brides wore cotton wedding dresses.

And Native Americans became great artisans in the preparation of animal skins for all kinds of clothes, moccasins, baskets, bags, tools, and tipis. Women wore the hides of buffalo, deer, antelope and elk. Though Indians didn't use tannic acid, they had ingenious methods for tanning skins, using animal and vegetable products. Their techniques required very hard labor, and the results were products of very high quality. White settlers marveled at the durability, softness, and light weight of the clothes and tipis. Men usually made the beads, but women worked them into designs for clothes and ornaments. Women often did embroidery, too, with porcupine quills, the use of which required great patience and technical mastery, for designing bags and pouches, clothes and moccasins. Some pieces were made to order—that is, the men told the women which designs to custom tailor to the men's individual tastes.

Native American women enjoyed fashionable accessories. They adored beads, shells, feathers, all types of decorations, and the more exotic the better, to enhance their clothing and hair ornaments. "They were style conscious," summed up John Upton Terrell and Donna M. Terrell.[1]

"From the far north came beads of walrus ivory. From the eastern coast came beads made from clam, oyster, quahog and periwinkle shells. From the sub-tropical south came beads made of wood, as well as of many kinds of oddly shaped and high colored shells. From the Southeast and the Midwest came fresh water pearls. From the Pacific Coast came exquisite beads of dentalium, abalone, and olivella shells. From the Rocky Mountains and the northern Great Plains came beads of animal teeth, among them the highly valued milk teeth of the elk. From several regions came the claws of bears for pendants, and these were eagerly sought by tribes of the southern Great Plains and the southwest. From the pueblos came the famous beads of turquoise which so delighted all women," wrote the Terrells.

Native Americans also adorned their skins with tattoos and body paints; they turned animal fats and vegetable oils into hair and body oils, and grass and seeds into perfumes. Women loved bird trophies and feathers from regions far from their homes—for example, ivory billed woodpecker scalps and parakeet skins, and wild turkey feathers, and feathers from tropical birds from Mexico. "Feathers were good business anywhere," write the Terrells.

The Terrells also tell the charming story of the small Havasupai tribe, which was finally driven by stronger, more numerous tribes into an area of the Southwest. There they discovered a red ocher, which they began trading for other items they needed. Soon they became rich and famous among Native Americans for their high-priced red ocher used for cosmetics and ceremonial costumes.

Women used everything from bark and grass to animal skins for their clothing. And contrary to legend and lore, women *did* dress themselves, and usually their whole bodies, with distinctive differences in designs between the tribes. A few tribes even fancied hats woven of materials used for basketry.

They had divergent tastes in hairstyles, and women of different ages coifed their hair in styles appropriate for their age groups. Some women wore their hair in two masses or braids that fell in front of their shoulders. Others let their hair hang free down their backs, and cut bangs across their foreheads. One observer in the Great Plains noticed that young Sioux girls wore braids down their back and tied them with pendants, while post-pubescent girls wore their hair above their shoulders. Some women wore decorated headbands. Some wore one braid down their backs. And for the puberty ceremony, Hopi girls pulled their hair up into large whorls on each side of their heads. They may have been trying to imitate the shape of the squash blossom, that popular symbol of fertility. Some women never cut their hair at all and let it grow down past their knees.

Women found ways to tweeze their eyebrows with wooden implements or clam shells, and they painted their faces in symbolic, traditional, and individualist designs. In some tribes, women had large portions of their bodies tattooed, and in other tribes tattoos were kept to a minimum. Some designs seemed to mimic the designs painted on pottery and woven into baskets. Men usually did the tattoo work, using everything from sharp flint instruments to cactus spines as needles, and dabbling in black and red colors in particular, and sometimes blue, too. Of course, Native Americans in the modern world abandoned their customs and techniques for adorning their hair and bodies long ago.

BOOKS ON INDIAN JEWELRY:

Here's a list of some books on Indian jewelry. Some may be available in libraries and museums, particularly the Indian museums under the aegis of the Smithsonian Institution, and some books may be available directly from publishers. These are only a sampling of many books on the subject.

1. *Zuni Jewelry*, (1992), by Theda and Michael Bassman, Schiffer Publisher Ltd., 1469 Morstein Road, West Chester, Pennsylvania 19380. This book has exquisite illustrations of jewelry, such as a squash blossom necklace with matching earrings and a ring made of mother-of-pearl, tortoise shell, and coral. The publisher noted that a free catalogue was available, and the book could be purchased directly from the publisher and at bookstores.

2. *Indian Jewelry Making, Volumes I and II*, by Oscar T. Branson, Treasure Chest Publications, Inc., P.O. Box 5250, Tucson, Arizona 85703. Vol. I, 1977, and Vol. II, 1979. These books depict fine examples of squash blossom jewelry, which has been wrought in countless variations of the basic theme. The books also have illustrations of Hopi and Santa Clara Indian wedding jugs, and other miniature silver pottery.

3. *Indian Jewelry On The Market*, by Peter N. Schiffer, Schiffer Publishing Ltd., 77 Lower Valley

Road, Atglen, Pennsylvania 19310. The book has illustrations of beautiful, fine quality Hopi jewelry that is on display in galleries and sells for as much as $1200 and $1400 for necklaces, $90 for earrings, $80 for rings. This company has a free catalogue and also sells the book directly to customers and through bookstores.

4. *Fetishes and Carvings of the Southwest*, (1976), by Oscar T. Branson, Treasure Chest Publications, Inc., P.O. Box 5250, Tucson, Arizona 85703. Fetishes were usually carvings in the forms of living things, and they were regarded as lucky objects with the power to influence the destinies of their owners. The power resided in the spirit of the fetish, not in the fetish itself. This book has pictures of horses, bears, and fox fetishes, among other figures, made of varied materials including stone, and a horse carved out of an abalone shell. The book is out of print, but available in libraries with books on American Indian Jewelry. The publishing company has books in print on the subject.

5. *Zuni, A Village of Silversmiths*, (1996), by James Ostler, Marian Rodee, and Milford Nahohai; Zuni A: Shiva Publishing, the University of New Mexico.

This book, too, has magnificent examples of handmade Zuni jewelry in a variety of designs. It is estimated there are over 1,000 Zuni silversmiths working at their craft today.

6. *Dancing Colors: Paths of Native American Women*, (1992), compiled by C.J. Brafford and Laine Thom,

Chronicle Books, San Francisco. Though not a book on jewelry, this history book contains a fine photo of a Zuni squash blossom necklace, which was made by a father for his daughter at the time of her marriage. He told her that her children would surround her, and the necklace was the symbol of her fertility.

Helpful Hints for Including Indian Jewelry and Crafts in a Contemporary Wedding:

NATIVE American jewelry is usually for sale in stores in major American cities and of course at Indian powwows and in stores specializing in Indian arts and crafts. See the Information Resources page at the end of this book for places that can refer you to stores, jewelry makers, and other outlets for Native American jewelry.

Perhaps the bride and groom would want to wear some pieces of traditional jewelry. There are Native American artists and jewelry makers who could create wedding bands with traditional patterns and designs on them.

Even if the bride opts for a Western-style white wedding dress, she could easily wear Native American jewelry with it. Turquoise jewelry, in particular, would be striking against a white dress—not to mention the fact that it fulfills the requirement for "something blue."

A bride and groom may choose to give their wedding attendants (bridesmaids, flowergirls, groomsmen, and ushers) a piece of Native American jewelry as a gift. Bridesmaids would certainly enjoy bracelets or earrings, while groomsmen may enjoy hand-crafted belt buckles or silver and turquoise cuff-links, tie-pins, or money clips. Such gifts would also be perfect for parents and grandparents.

NOTE

1. *Indian Women of the Western Morning: Their Life in Early America*, by John Upton Terrell and Donna M. Terrell, The Dial Press, New York, 1974, and Anchor Books, New York, 1976.

Post Script —
Divorce and
Remarriage

Fools Crow, the Teton Sioux Indian, who became engaged and married to his wife, Fannie, in a short period of time—perhaps as little as one night—in South Dakota, simply by collecting her possessions and taking them to his own camp, became a widower in 1954 after 38 years in a happy marriage. For four years, he lived alone as a bachelor. But one day, the daughter of a friend of his came to him and said her mother, Kate, a widow, was lonely. Her family thought it would be a very good idea if Fools Crow married her. Wasn't he ever lonely? Kate's daughter wanted to know. Yes, he was, he said.

And so he decided to marry Kate; with her he lived very happily, too. She had never been off the reservation; he began to take her traveling, and she enjoyed the adventure. Fools Crow's marriages were blessedly unmarred by any kind of strife. In recounting the tale of his second marriage to Thomas E. Mails for the book, *Fools Crow*, he leaves out any mention of a wedding feast or a bride price. These rites rarely came up for second marriages unless the brides were still quite young. In Kate's case, she was already well into middle age, and so was Fools Crow.

Not all Indians enjoyed such serene domestic lives. Divorce was a fairly common practice among Native Americans. Some tribes, such as the Oglala Sioux, had rather complicated procedures for divorce, but most divorces were simple affairs, or they could be. A woman put her husband's possessions outside the house. Or the woman went home to her own family. Or the man simply left home one day and never returned.

In some tribes, women remarried many times, either because they were divorced or widowed. Each time they remarried, of course, they didn't have to go through all the elaborate gift giving and mighty preparations as they had done for their first marriages. And the older a woman was, the less complicated the customs and traditions were. Everyone just wanted to be happy.

For further reading about family customs, structures, and traditions of Native Americans, see the bibliography at the end of this book.

BIBLIOGRAPHY AND INFORMATION RESOURCES

Axtell, James, editor. *The Indian Peoples of Eastern America: A Documentary History of the Sexes*. The College of William and Mary, Oxford University Press: New York and Oxford, 1981.

Bailey, Flora L., *Some Sex Beliefs and Practices in a Navaho Community*. Cambridge, The Museum, 1950. This is a rare book available in some Harvard University libraries and at the National Museum of the American Indian in New York.

Brafford, C.J., and Thom, Laine, compilers, *Dancing Colors: Paths of Native American Women*. Chronicle Books: San Francisco, 1992.

Driver, Harold E., *Indians of North America*, 2nd edition, Revised. University of Chicago Press: Chicago and London, 1961, 1969.

Ewers, John C., *The Blackfeet: Raiders of the Northwestern Plains*. University of Oklahoma Press: Norman, 1958.

An Ethnology Dictionary of the Navaho Language. The Franciscan Fathers, publishers: Saint Michaels, Arizona, 1910.

Hill, Sarah H., *Weaving New Worlds*. University of North Carolina Press: Chapel Hill and London, 1997.

Hoxie, Frederick E., editor. *Encyclopedia of North American Indians*. Houghton Mifflin Company: Boston, New York, 1996.

Krupat, Arnold, editor. *Native American Autobiography: an Anthology*. The University of Wisconsin Press: Wisconsin, 1994.

Mails, Thomas E. *Fools Crow*. University of Nebraska Press: Lincoln, 1979.

Mankiller, Wilma, and Wallis, Michael. *Mankiller: A Chief and Her People* (an autobiography of Wilma Mankiller, a chief of the Cherokee Nation). St. Martin's Press: New York, 1993.

Mooney, James. *Myths of the Cherokee and Sacred Formulas of the Cherokees*. Charles and Randy Elder-Booksellers, Publishers: Nashville, Tennessee, 1982.

Niethammer, Carolyn. *Daughters of the Earth: The Lives and Legends of American Indian Women*. Touchstone: New York, 1977.

Page, Susanne and Jake, *Hopi*. Abradale Press and Harry N. Abrams, Inc.: New York, 1982.

——*Navajo*. Harry N. Abrams Publishers: New York, 1995.

Rasmussen, William M. S., and Tilton, Robert S. *Pocahontas: Her Life and Legend*. Virginia Historical Society: Richmond, Virginia, 1994.

Handbook of the North American Indian. Smithsonian Institution.

Spittal, Wm. Guy, editor. *Iroquois Women: An Anthology*. Iroqrafts, Ltd., Iroquois Publications: Ontario, Canada, 1990, 1996.

Stockel, H. Henrietta. *Women of the Apache Nation*. University of Nevada Press: Reno, Nevada, 1991.

Terrell, John Upton, and Terrell, Donna M. *Indian Women of the Western Morning*. Dial Press: New York, 1974 and Anchor Books: New York, 1976.

Time-Life Editor. *The Woman's Way*. Time-Life Books: Alexandria, Virginia 1995.

Trigger, Bruce G., and Washburn, Wilcomb E. *Cambridge History of the Native Peoples of the Americas*, Vols. 1 and 2. Cambridge University Press: New York, 1996.

Walker, James R. *Lakota Society*. University of Nebraska Press: Lincoln and London, and the Colorado Historical Society, 1982.

Witherspoon, Gary. *Navajo Kinship and Marriage*. University of Chicago Press: Chicago, London, 1975. Also see *Chapter 11: Fashions, Jewelry, Basketry, Cloth Weaving, and Decorations* for the books on Jewelry.

INFORMATION RESOURCES:

1. American Indian Community House, 212-598-0100. 708 Broadway, New York, N.Y. 10003.

2. National Museum of the American Indian, 212-514-3700. One Bowling Green, New York 10004. This museum is under the auspices of the Smithsonian Institution.

3. The Cultural Resources Center, Sutland, Maryland, is scheduled to open with a great deal of exhibition space in Fall 1999. This center is also under the auspices of the Smithsonian Institution.

4. The Mall Museum, Washington, D.C., is scheduled to open in the year 2000. This, too, is under the auspices of the Smithsonian Institution.

5. Louis Mofsie, founder and leader of the Thunderbird American Indian Dancers, teaches dance and beadwork at the American Indian Community House, 708 Broadway, New York, N.Y. 10003. Call the American Indian Community House, 212-598-0100, or the National Museum of the American Indian, 212-514-3700, for information about his scheduled performances and classes.

INDEX

A

Abenaki tribe, 141

Acorns, 131

Adoption ceremony, 84

Adultery, 14

African Americans, 117

Alaska, 118

Alaska powwow, 125

Aleut tribe, 118

Algonquin tribe, "The Bride's Song," 27

American Indian Community House in New York City, 71, 115, 165

American Indian Exposition, 127

American Indian Love Lyrics and Other Verse (Barnes), 46-47, 48

American Indian Myths and Legends, 31

American Indian Prose and Poetry (Levitas, Vivelo, and Vivelo), 47, 48

American Indians. *See* Native Americans

Animal skin preparation, 148, 150

Animal teeth, 151

Antelope, 132, 150

Apache tribe, 16, 103-108

foods of, 136

"Mountain Spirit Dance of the Apaches," 116

B

Ball-throwing Rite, 87
Bar mitzvah, 92
Barnes, Nellie, *American Indian Love Lyrics and Other Verse,* 46-47, 48
Basket-making, 148, 149
  for boiling food, 131, 149
Bassman, Theda and Michael, *Zuni Jewelry,* 154
Bat mitzvah, 92
Beads, 151
Berries, 131
Bird trophies and feathers, 152
Birth ceremonies, 54
Bison, 132
Blackfoot tribe
  and magic charms, 13-14, 19
  polygamy in, 10-11
  sexual experimentation in, 93
Blanket and wedding vase in Cherokee tribe tradition, 70, 73
Body paint, 152
Bow ties, 149
Brafford, C.J., and Laine Thom, *Dancing Colors: Path of Native American Women,* 155-156
Branson, Oscar T. *Fetishes and Carvings of the Southwest,* 155

Indian Jewelry Making, Volumes I and II, 154
Bridegrooms and mothers-in-law, 17, 68, 78
"The Bride's Song" (Algonquin tribe), 27
Brule Sioux tribe, "The Legend of the Flute," 31-38
Buffalo, 132, 150
Buffalo blood broth, 132
Buffalo Ceremony, 87
Bundles in Hopi wedding traditons, 53
Burial robes, 17, 54, 57

C

Cannibalism, 109
Carson, Dale, *New Native American Cooking,* 137-143
Centerpieces, 144
Ceramics, 149
Chastity belts, 87
Cherokee tribe, 141
  marriage arrangements, 71
  as matrilineal, 57, 69
  Sioux bridegroom and Cherokee bride, 69-74
  wood gifts, 71-72
Child custody traditions, 11, 52, 58, 84, 85-86
Children in the wedding ceremony, 54, 56, 59
Chippewa tribe, 28

Chono, Maria, 95-102, 112, 136
Christianity
  marriage traditions, 62
  religious conversions, 4-5
Circle dance, 116-117, 120
Citizenship granted to Native
  Americans, 62
Clan membership, 49-50, 52,
  69, 76
  See also Incest
Clowns, 107
Coloring designs, 150, 152
Commercialization
  and Iroquois tribe, 75
  of Native American arts
  and crafts, 148-149
  at powwows, 122, 149
Common law marriages, 57
Consomme of Trout, 136
Cookbooks, 137
Coral jewelry, 148
Corn, 144
  in Hopi traditions, 55, 59
  ways of preparing, 130
  wild, 129
Cornmeal
  in the Hopi wedding
  ceremony, 56
  in the Navajo wedding
  ceremony, 63-64, 67
Cosmetics, 152
Courtship
  circle dance, 116-117
  general Indian traditions,
  12-17, 93

grooming of men, 87-88
Lakota-Oglala Sioux, 81-82
  See also Puberty
  celebrations
Cradles, 87
Cree tribe, magic charms,
  13, 19
Crib boards, 6
Crow tribe, Crow Fair
  powwow, 126
Cuban puberty celebrations, 92
Cultural erosion and
  eradication, 8-9, 62, 153
Cultural Resources Center,
  Smithsonian
  Institution, 165
Cummerbunds, 149

D
Dakota tribe, "Love Song," 26
Dances. *See* Powwows
*Dancing Colors: Path of Native
  American Women*
  (Brafford and Thom),
  155-156
Dancing contests, 106, 122
Debutante balls, 15, 92
Deer, 132, 150
Densmore, Frances, *Poems
  form Sioux and Chippewa
  Songs,* 28, 30
Divorce, 11, 52, 57-58, 70, 85,
  86, 160
Dress for weddings. *See*
  Wedding clothes

Dried Corn Soup, 135
Drums and rattles, 117

E

Elk, 132, 150
Elopement, 14, 88
Embroidery, 150
Equality of Indian men and
    women, 12, 57, 65
Eskimos, 118, 125
*An Ethnology Dictionary of the
    Navajo Language*
    (Franciscan Brothers), 67

F

Face painting, 81, 84, 153
Fancy Dance, 120
Fannie and Fools Crow, 50-51
Fashion wear, 149
Fashions, jewelry, basketry,
    cloth weaving, and
    decorations, 147-158
Fasting, 109-110
Feathers, 151, 152
Fertility symbols, 15, 63, 153,
    156
*Fetishes and Carvings of the
    Southwest* (Branson), 155
Fish recipes, 141
Flute music, 13, 47, 82, 88,
    117
Folklore, 33-48
Food, 129-145
Fools Crow, 50-51, 159-160

Fools Crow (Mails), 50-51,
    52, 160
Fort Sill Apache Tribal
    Complex, 103
Franciscan Brothers, *An
    Ethnology Dictionary of
    the Navajo Language,* 67
Fresh water pearls, 151
Fry bread, 104-105, 142

G

Gallup Ceremonial
    (powwow), 126
Game birds, 133
Game dishes, 141
Gathering of Nations
    Powwow, 126
George Gustav Heye
    Center, 47
"Give-aways," 122
Gourd Dance, 120, 121, 122
Grass Dance, 120

H

Hairstyles, 59, 64, 83, 99, 103,
    108, 152-153
Hand painting, 84
Hand washing ceremony
    tradition of the Navajo
    tribe, 64, 67
Happily May I Walk
    (Hirschfelder), 121
Hassrick, Royal B., *The Sioux:
    Life and Customs of A
    Warrior Society,* 90

Hats, 152
Havasupai tribe, 152
Health care benefits, 70
"The Heart's Friend"
    (Shoshone tribe), 30-31
"Heathens," 5
Helpful hints
    Cherokee tradition for a
        modern wedding, 70, 73
    Hopi traditions for a
        modern wedding, 59
    incorporating traditional
        dances and music into
        the modern wedding,
        124
    Iroquois tradition for a
        modern wedding, 77, 79
    jewelry and crafts in a con-
        temporary wedding,
        157-158
    Lakota-Oglala Sioux
        tradition for a modern
        wedding, 89
    Native American cuisine
        for a wedding dinner,
        144-145
    Navajo traditions for a
        modern wedding, 67-68
    old traditons for contempo-
        rary life, 19
    poetry and folklore for a
        modern wedding
        ceremony, 46-48
"Her Shadow" (Ojibwa tribe),
    23-24

Hill, Sarah H., *Weaving*
    New Worlds:
    Southeastern Cherokee
    Women and Their
    Basketry, 71-72
Hirschfelder, Arlene, *Happily*
    May I Walk, 121
History, 9
Hodge, F.W., 22
Home decoration, 149
Hopi (Page, Susanne and
    Jake), 56
Hopi tribe, 16
    bride price, 50
    foods of, 133
    male weavers in, 150
    as matrilineal, 52, 55, 57
    puberty ceremony, 153
    traditions for a modern
        wedding, 59
    wedding and burial
        dresses, 17, 54
    wedding customs, 53-60
Horses as gift items in
    marriage agreements, 8,
    65, 68
Hunting and gathering tribes,
    10, 13, 17

I

"I Am Arrayed Like the
    Roses," 29
"I Sit Here Thinking of Her,"
    28-29

Incest, 10, 49-50, 69
    See also Clan membership
Indian Country
    Communications, 128
Indian Jewelry Making,
    Volumes I and II
    (Branson), 154
Indian Jewelry on the Market
    (Schiffer), 154-155
Indian Women of the Western
    Morning (Terrell, John
    Lipton and Donna M.),
    132, 151
Indians. *See* Native
    Americans
Iroquois tribe
    as matrilineal, 57, 75-76
    privacy of, 9, 75
    wedding customs, 75-79
Iroquois Women: An
    Anthology, 78

J

James I, king of England, 4
Jazz and Native Americans,
    56, 117
Jewelry, 148-149, 151
    books on, 154-156
    in a contemporary
        wedding, 157-158
    turquoise, 63, 147, 148,
        151, 157
Jewish bar mitzvah and bat
    mitzvah, 92

K

Kate and Fools Crow, 159-160
Kidnapping women for
    brides, 81

L

Lakota Society (Walker), 90
Lakota tribe, 33, 90
Lakota-Oglala Sioux tribe
    divorce procedures, 160
    tradition for a modern
        wedding, 89
    wedding customs, 81-90
Land benefits, 70
"The Legend of the Flute"
    (Brule Sioux tribe),
    31-38, 47
Legends and myths, 31-48
Levitas, Gloria, Frank
    Robert Vivelo, and
    Jacqueline J. Vivelo,
    American Indian Prose
    and Poetry, 47, 48
Life cycle rituals, 117
Literature, 21-48
Little House, 96, 98
Long House, 9
Love poems, 21-31
Love potions, 13, 28, 87, 111
"Love Song" (Dakota
    tribe), 26
"Lover's Wooing" or
    "Blanket Song" (Zuni
    tribe), 24-26

M

McManus, Jill, "The Sounds of Hopi," 56
Magic charms, 13, 30
Mails, Thomas E., *Fools Crow,* 50-51, 52, 160
Mall Museum, Washington, D.C., Smithsonian Institution, 165
Maple-Mustard Vinaigrette, 140
Marriage
  adaptation to, 17, 93
  age for, 12
  arranged, 10, 51-52
  between Indians, 6
  between Indians and whites, 1-7
  bride prices, 8, 50, 57, 65-67, 72, 76, 82, 83, 160
  as business deals, 2, 92
  contracted, 8
  erosion of traditions, 8-9
  feast traditions, 8, 116
  general Indian traditions, 8-18
  gifts exchanged in, 6, 8, 50, 71, 92, 112
  Powhatan tribe traditions, 8
  sexual relations in, 17
  variety of traditions, 9-10
  See also Native Americans; Tribal wedding customs
Massachusetts powwow, 125
Matrilineal tradition, 1, 52, 57, 69, 75-76, 85

Meat, 131, 132
Medicine tipi, 104, 105
Men's work, 10
Menstruation
  courtship and marriage advice, 15
  fables and superstitions about, 16, 91, 95
  isolation in special housing, 107, 110
  and marriage, 12, 86, 111
  scratching sticks, 111
  See also Puberty celebration
Menu cards, 144
Mescalero Apache Reservation, 103
Mofsie, Louis, 105, 115, 116, 121, 165
Monogamy, 11, 76, 85
Montana powwow, 119, 126
Mooney, James, *Myths of the Cherokee and Sacred Formulas of the Cherokees,* 71
Moral tales, 31
Mothers-in-law, 17, 68, 78
"Mountain Spirit Dance of the Apaches," 116
Mud battles in Hopi wedding tradition, 55, 56
Mushrooms Stuffed with Mishquammauquock (salmon), 138-139

Myths of the Cherokee and Sacred Formulas of the Cherokees (Mooney), 71

N

National Museum of the American Indian in New York, Smithsonian Institution, 9, 47, 78, 115, 116, 147, 149, 154, 165
Native American Antipasto, 140-141
Native American Autobiography: An Anthology (Underhill), 95-102, 112
Native American Hominy Soup, 134-135
Native Americans
  arts and crafts, 122, 149
  citizenship granted to, 62
  cultural erosion and eradication, 8-9, 62, 153
  cultural preservation, 115, 120
  demographics of, 118
  history of, 9
  and jazz, 56, 117
  languages of, 119
  music and singing of, 117
  rituals of, 22
  as servicemen, 121
  See also Marriage; Pan-Indian culture; Tribal wedding customs

Natural world, 31
Navajo (Page, Susanne and Jake), 61, 63, 68
Navajo tribe
  band, 106
  bride price, 50
  jewely-making, 148
  language as spy code, 121
  legend about sex, 11-12
  as matrilineal, 52, 57
  puberty rites of passage, 108
  squaw dances of, 15
  traditions for a modern wedding, 67-68
  wedding customs, 61-68
New Mexico powwows, 119, 126-127
New Native American Cooking (Carson), 137-143
New York powwow, 125
New York Public Library, 46
Nightcrawling, 15-16
Nikoa, 69-74
North Dakota powwow, 127

O

Oglala Sioux tribe. *See* Lakota-Oglala Sioux tribe
Ojibwa tribe, "Her Shadow," 23-24
Oklahoma powwows, 119, 127-128
Old traditons for contemporary (modern) life, 19

Omaha tribe, 119
Oral histories, 9
Ostler, James, Marian Rodee,
   and Milford Nahohai,
   *Zuni, A Village of
   Silversmiths,* 155

P

Page, Susanne and Jake
   Hopi, 56
   Navajo, 61, 63, 68
Pan-Indian culture, 120
   See also Native Americans
Papago tribe, 94, 95-103
Parades, 106
Party favor books, 145
Patrilineal tradition, 52
Pawnee tribe, 32, 119
Peace of Pocahantas, 2-3
Perfumes, 152
Plains tribes, 119, 120, 121, 122
Pocahantas, *See also* Rolfe,
   Rebecca
Pocahontas, 1-7
*Poems from Sioux and
   Chippewa Songs*
   (Densmore), 28, 30
Poetry and folklore for a
   modern wedding
   ceremony, 46-48
Polygamy, 10-11, 29, 85
Porcupine quills, 150
Powhatan, Chief, 1, 2, 8, 11
Powhatan tribe, 1-7
Powwow Directory, 128

Powwows, 9, 115-128
   commercialization at,
      122, 149
   jewelry and crafts at, 157
   locations of, 124-128
Premarital sex, 15
   See also Sexual
      experimentation
Private traditions, 9, 75, 103,
   116, 120
Promiscuity, 87, 93
Prostitutes, 65
Psychological transition for
   newlyweds, 17
Puberty celebrations, 83-84,
   91-113
   "Mountain Spirit Dance of
      the Apaches," 116
   See also Courtship;
      Menstruation
Pueblo tribe, 71

R

Radin, Paul, *The Winnebago
   Tribe,* 109
Recipes
   Consomme of Trout, 136
   Dried Corn Soup, 135
   Frybread, 142-143
   Maple-Mustard Vinaigrette,
      140
   Mushrooms Stuffed with
      Mishquammauquock
      (salmon), 138-139

Native American
    Antipasto, 140-141
Native American Hominy
    Soup, 134-135
Red Earth powwow, 128
Red ocher, 152
Relatives. *See* Clan
    memberships; Incest
Remarriage, 159-160
Reservations, 70, 118
Rodeos, 103-104
Rolfe, John, 1-3, 5-7
Rolfe, Rebecca, 5-7
    See also Pocahantas
Rolfe, Thomas, 6, 7
Round dance, 116-117, 120, 121
Ryan, Georgetta, 147

S

Schiffer, Peter N., *Indian
    Jewelry on the Market*,
    154-155
Scratching sticks, 111
Separation of the sexes, 12-13,
    16, 17, 94
"The Serpent of the Sea"
    (Zuni tribe), 38-45, 47
Servicemen, 121
Sexual experimentation, 14,
    93
    See also Premarital sex
Sexual relations in marriage,
    17
Shakopee reserve, 70
Shells, 151
Shinnecock tribe powwow,
    119, 125
Shoshone tribe, "The Heart's
    Friend," 30-31
Silver jewelry, 148
Singing, 117
*The Sioux: Life and Customs of
    A Warrior Society*
    (Hassrick), 90
Sioux tribe, 28, 92, 119, 122
    hairstyles, 153
    Sioux bridegroom and
        Cherokee bride, 69-74
Smith, Captain John, 3
Smithsonian Institution
    Cultural Resources
        Center, 165
    Mall Museum, Washington,
        D.C., 165
    National Museum of the
        American Indian in
        New York, 9, 47, 78, 115,
        116, 147, 149, 154, 165
Songs and chants of tribal
    life, 22
"The Sounds of Hopi"
    (McManus), 56
Soups, 141
Spell casting, 13
Spinsters, 18
Squash blossom, 153
Squash blossom necklaces,
    15, 63, 156
Squaw dance, 15, 116-117, 120

Stockel, Henrietta, *Women of the Apache Nation,* 103
Succotash, 130, 141-142
Survival tactics, 9, 78

T

Tablecloths, 144
Tattoos, 152, 153
Terrell, John Lipton and Donna M., *Indian Women of the Western Morning,* 132, 151
Teton Sioux tribe, 50-51, 159
Theater for the New City in New York City, 115-116
Thohono O'odham tribe, 95
Thunderbird American Indian Dancers, 105, 115, 116, 120, 165
Tipis, 84-85, 121
  medicine, 104, 105
Tribal governments, 57
Tribal wedding customs, 49-90
  background, 49-52
  Hopi tribe, 53-60
  Iroquois tribe, 75-79
  Lakota-Oglala Sioux, 81-90
  Navajo tribe, 61-68
  Sioux bridegroom and Cherokee bride, 69-74
  See also Marriage; Native Americans
Tribe's census, 84
Turquoise jewelry, 63, 147, 148, 151, 157

U

Underhill, Ruth, *Native American Autobiography: An Anthology,* 95-102, 112
United States Cavalry, 32
United States Census, 118
United Tribes Technical College powwow, 119, 127

V

Veterans, 121
Virginia Company, 7
Virginity, 13, 15, 16, 93

W

Walker, James R., *Lakota Society,* 90
Walrus ivory, 151
Wampanoag tribe powwow, 119, 125
War bundles, 110
Wards of the state, 62
Wars and widows, 17-18
Weaving, 148
  by males, 17, 54, 148, 150
Weaving New Worlds: Southeastern Cherokee Women and Their Basketry (Hill), 71-72
Wedding cakes in the Iroquois tradition, 77, 79
Wedding clothes, 147
  in Hopi ceremonies, 17, 54, 56, 57, 59

in Lakota-Oglala Sioux
    ceremonies, 83-84
Whittaker, Reverend
    Alexander, 4, 5
Widowers, 159
Widows, 17-18, 160
Wild corn, 129
Winnebago tribe, 109-112
The Winnebago Tribe
    (Radin), 109
Women of the Apache Nation
    (Stockel), 103
Women's work, 10
World Eskimo Indian
    Olympics, 125

Z

Zuni, A Village of Silversmiths
    (Ostler, Rodee, and
    Nahohai), 155
Zuni Jewelry (Bassman, Theda
    and Michael), 154
Zuni tribe
    jewelry-making by, 148
    "Lover's Wooing" or
        "Blanket Song," 24-26
    "The Serpent of the Sea,"
        38-45
    squash blossom
        necklace, 156